W0016719

Civil Service Reform: Strengthening World Bank and IMF Collaboration

THE WORLD BANK
Washington, D.C.

A discussion paper prepared by the Public Sector Group of the World Bank's PREM Network and the Fiscal Affairs Department of the IMF.

Library of Congress Cataloging-in-Publication Data

Civil service reform: strengthening World Bank and IMF collaboration / World Bank, International Monetary Fund.
        p. cm. – (Directions in development)
    Includes bibliographical references.
    ISBN 0-8213-5095-1

    1. International Monetary Fund. 2. World Bank. 3. International finance. 4. Development banks. I. World Bank. II. International Monetary Fund. III. Series.

HG3881.5. W57 C478 2001
351—dc21

                                                                2002016816

Cover photo by Adalberto Pacheco

Contents

Tables

Figures

Foreword

Civil service reform is often essential to bring about governance improvements that are needed for sustainable poverty reduction. On September 6, 2001, staff of the World Bank and International Monetary Fund (IMF, or Fund) met at a workshop co-sponsored by the IMF's Fiscal Affairs Department (FAD) and the Public Sector Group of the World Bank's Poverty Reduction and Economic Management (PREM) Network to discuss the support for civil service reform offered by their respective institutions. Several key conclusions emerged from that workshop. First, strengthened collaboration between the World Bank and the IMF should ensure consistency between the sometimes-conflicting goals of short-term fiscal discipline and longer-term structural reforms supported by Fund and Bank programs. Second, realistic objectives embedded in a medium-term fiscal framework, explicit assumptions about sequencing and timing of reforms, and continuing assessment of the underlying political feasibility of reforms are crucial for effective civil service reform. Finally, the maintenance of a minimum core set of wage and employment data is indispensable to have a full understanding of the public sector and its potential maladies.

The workshop was organized in response to concerns raised during a joint trip to Africa in 2001 by the World Bank president and the IMF managing director. Clearly, efforts to support civil service reform, with some notable exceptions, had not been very successful over the years, particularly in poor countries. As a result, FAD and PREM decided to review the experiences of Bank-Fund advice to countries in the area of civil service reform, and to draw lessons for the future. The workshop was organized in the context of other discussions aimed at strengthening Bank-Fund collaboration on country programs and streamlining conditionality.

About 60 staff, including managers and country teams from the two institutions, participated in the discussions. In advance of the workshop, an issues paper was prepared by Bank and Fund staff to guide the

discussions.[1] The present paper includes the background material prepared for the workshop, as well as the resulting conclusions and next
steps proposed.

Teresa Ter-Minassian   Cheryl Gray
Director, Fiscal Affairs Department   Director, Public Sector Group
International Monetary Fund   Poverty Reduction and
                                       Economic Management Network

March 2002

Acknowledgments

This paper was prepared by the staffs of the Public Sector Group of the World Bank and the FAD of the IMF, under the direction of Cheryl Gray, then Public Sector Director in the World Bank and Sanjeev Gupta, Assistant Director of the IMF FAD.

The primary authors were Nick Manning and Jeffrey Rinne, PREM, World Bank; and Sanjeev Gupta, Calvin McDonald, Gabriela Inchauste, and Juan Pablo Cordoba, FAD, IMF. Amar Bhattacharya, Stefan Koeberle, Helen Sutch, and Ulrich Zachau of the World Bank made valuable contributions.

The preparation of the paper was made possible by the contributions of country teams in the Bank and the Fund who provided the detailed background material for the case studies. Key contributions were received from:

	World Bank	IMF
Benin	Mouhamadou Drame, Catherine M. Laurent, Claude Leroy-Themeze	Cyrille Briancon, Fabien Nsengiyumva
Bolivia	Pablo Alonso	Wayne Lewis, María González
Cambodia	Su Yong Song, Toshi Kato	Thomas Rumbaugh, Philippe Marciniak
FYR of Macedonia	Pascale Kervyn de Lettenhove, Gary Reid	Biswajit Banerjee, Juan Zalduendo
Mali	Ezzeddine Moudoud, Mohamed A. Touré, Christina A. Wood	Dhaneshwar Ghura, Diarietou Gaye
Mongolia	Vera Songwe	Lazaros Molho, Vincent Moissinac

	World Bank	**IMF**
Pakistan	Ahmad Ahsan, Christine Allison	Klaus Enders, Gunther Taube, Valeria Fichera
Russian Federation	Neil Parison	Thomas Laursen, Ali Mansoor
Tanzania	Denyse Morin	Jurgen Reitmaier, Harry Snoek
Republic of Yemen	Linda van Gelder, Amine Khene, Giulio de Tommaso	Edward Gardner, David Moore
Zambia	Mushiba Nyamazana, Harry Garnett	Robert Sharer, Koshy Mathai

Suzanne Alavi (FAD, IMF) and Claudia Nolan (PREM, World Bank) provided administrative support for organizing the workshop. Kim Kelley, with the World Bank's Office of the Publisher, was the production editor for this publication.

Acronyms and Abbreviations

APL	Adaptable program loan
AsDB	Asian Development Bank
BOP	Balance of payments
BESSIP	Basic Education Subsector Investment Program Support Project (World Bank)
CAS	Country Assistance Strategy
CCM	Chama Cha Mapinduzi (Revolutionary Party) of Tanzania
CSF	Civil service fund
EFF	Extended Fund Facility
ESAF	Enhanced structural adjustment facility
FAD	Fiscal Affairs Department
FNRB	Fonds National de Retraite du Bénin
GDP	Gross domestic product
GoP	Government of Pakistan
HIPC	Heavily Indebted Poor Countries
IFI	International financial institution
IMF	International Monetary Fund (or the Fund)
IT	Information technology
LCU	Local currency units
LGO	Local governments (Pakistan)
MDAs	Ministries, departments, and agencies

MoCS	Ministry of the civil service (Benin)
MOCSAR	Ministry of Civil Service and Administrative Reform (Republic of Yemen)
MoF	Ministry of finance
MTEF	Medium-term expenditure framework
MTPS	Medium-term pay strategy
PER	Public Expenditure Review
PIU	Project implementation unit
PMG	Priority Mission Group
PRGF	Poverty Reduction and Growth Facility
PRSC	Poverty Reduction Support Credit
PRSP	Poverty Reduction Strategy Paper
PSCAP	Public Sector Capacity-Building Project (World Bank)
PSMAC	Public Sector Management Adjustment Credit/Loan (for the former Yugoslav Republic of Macedonia)
SASE	Selected accelerated salary enhancement
SBA	Stand-by arrangement
TCAP	Technical Cooperation Action Plan
UTS	Unified tariff schedule

I
Introduction

This paper sets out the principal aspects of civil service reform that were discussed at a workshop for World Bank and International Monetary Fund (IMF, or the Fund) staff on September 6, 2001.[2] The objective of the workshop was to strengthen collaboration between the Bank and the Fund in order to achieve greater effectiveness in Bank- and Fund-supported programs in this area. About 60 staff, including managers and country teams, participated in the discussions. Both institutions recognize the centrality of a competent, affordable, and accountable public administration. The central question is how to bring this about.

The Bank-Fund workshop was the second thematic discussion held by Bank and Fund staff in the context of recent discussions on strengthening Bank-Fund collaboration on country programs and conditionality.[3] The principles noted in the recently established Joint Guidelines include: clarity on primary responsibilities, full consultations between institutions, and distinct accountability in lending decisions. The Fund's primary responsibility is to ensure macroeconomic stability, and the Bank's core mandate is to help countries reduce poverty, particularly by focusing on the institutional, structural, and social dimensions of development. When conditionality in structural areas such as civil service reform is judged critical to success in Fund-supported programs, the Guidelines note that collaboration must ensure that conditionality is consistent with the medium-term reforms covered in the country's dialogue with the Bank.

Section II presents an overview of the major objectives of civil service reform, highlighting some of the core macrofiscal and structural perspectives. Section III follows, and highlights recent Bank- and Fund-supported programs that address civil service reform. Section IV considers the effectiveness of Bank and Fund interventions, noting the intrinsic tensions between reform objectives and the politically challenging nature of civil service reforms.

Section V considers how the two organizations have worked, both individually and in tandem. The discussion is informed by 11 country case studies.[4] Section V also offers conclusions and proposals for improving the effectiveness of Bank-Fund interventions in civil service reform.

Annex 1 briefly summarizes the elements of civil service reforms in Bank- and Fund-supported programs during 1999 and 2000, while Annex 2 provides the case studies and briefly describes the size and structure of the civil service, recent structural and institutional reforms, and the relationship between these reforms and macroeconomic stability and sustainability.

This paper is not a comprehensive primer on best practices in civil service reform. It presents the views of Bank and Fund staff that gathered to discuss this important issue, and is intended to foster further dialogue. The focus of the paper, like that of the joint workshop in September 2001, is on civilian central government, including the central executive and legislative administrations.[5] Civil service reform should be assessed in the context of overall public expenditure management, government reform, and improvements in governance, not simply in terms of reform of government *employment*. That broader context includes a country's economic, social, and political institutions, in particular the relationship between central and subnational government. These larger contextual points are acknowledged, but are not analyzed in this document.

II

The Goals of
Civil Service Reform

Reforming the civil service is not a goal in its own right. Moreover, there is no single best "model" of public administration. Given vested interests that must be confronted, civil service reforms must be justified to policymakers and the public by their impact on poverty and on the effectiveness of government—either directly in terms of service delivery, or indirectly through their impact on macroeconomic stability or improved economic and social policy formulation and implementation.

In many countries oversized public sectors arise from an anachronistic government policy that has yet to address fully the changing orientation of the economy. In countries where public services are produced inefficiently or where the government is excessively large, fiscal pressures may emanate from the wage bill or from inappropriate purchases of goods and services. Meanwhile, structural deficiencies may reduce the quality of public services, create improper incentives in public employment, and limit the government's ability to pursue equitable public policies.

While the ultimate goals are to reduce poverty and enhance government effectiveness, civil service reforms generally target more specific objectives. These range from objectives that are primarily structural—with an impact on service delivery and government effectiveness—to objectives that have a more direct link to macroeconomic stability. Figure 1 offers a stylized representation of objectives found in civil service reform programs.

In practice, there is no easy divide between structural and macrofiscal concerns in civil service reform, since each directly impacts the other. The structural issues of employment and career path, pay policy, and organizational arrangements are key to improved accountability and service delivery, but can also have a significant fiscal impact. In turn, a relatively high civil service wage bill can threaten macroeconomic stability; but measures to reduce the wage bill can have important structural effects.

Macrofiscal and structural concerns lie behind the involvement of both the Bank and the Fund in all countries. However, the relative importance

Figure 1 Typical Objectives of Civil Service Reform Programs

Correct fiscal imbalances: • Wage bill relative to gross domestic product (GDP) and as a proportion of government expenditures • Sustainability of civil service pension system	Potential impact on macroeconomic stability
Pay and career structures: • Wage levels and comparability with private sector • Promotion and career structures • Shortages of qualified labor in particular skills areas	
Improving accountability and service delivery: • Reducing high-level corruption and partisan influence • Creating incentives for senior staff • Reducing administrative corruption • Service delivery improvements in key sectors, particularly health and education • Improved capacity for regulation and revenue-raising • Empowering consumer groups through surveys and reform of administrative laws	Structural issues with potential impact on service delivery

Source: Bank-Fund staff.

of these issues varies significantly by country, as the 11 selected country cases demonstrate (see Table 1).

Fiscal Stability and Sustainability Concerns in the Country Cases

The size of the wage bill can threaten macroeconomic stability, and as such continues to be a key issue in many countries (see Table 2). Of the 11 case studies, Fund and Bank mission teams identified this as a particular concern in five countries (Bolivia, the former Yugoslav Republic of Macedonia, Mongolia, the Republic of Yemen, and Zambia). Although these are among the countries with the largest wage bills as a proportion of GDP or of total government expenditure, the size of the wage bill is not necessarily the only indicator of risk to macrofiscal stability. The level of other public expenditures, as well as the size and sustainability of the overall revenue effort, is equally critical.

While the wage bill has contracted in the past in several countries, pressures remain to increase spending, principally because of the low level of wages, political pressures to extend public sector employment, poorly executed decentralization programs, and the need to retain staff in

Table 1 Issues Raised in Bank-Fund Programs

	Correct fiscal imbalances		Improve pay and career structure			Improve accountability and service delivery	
	Wage Bill	Pensions	Wage levels	Career structure	Improve skill levels	Reduce administrative corruption	Improve service delivery
Benin[1]		X		X			
Bolivia[1,2]			X	X	X		
Cambodia			X	X		X	X
Macedonia, FYR	X		X	X			X
Mali[1]		X		X		X	X
Mongolia	X		X		X		X
Pakistan		X	X	X		X	X
Russian Federation			X	X			
Tanzania[1]	X						
Yemen, Rep. of[1,3]	X	X	X			X	X
Zambia[1]					X	X	X

1. Heavily Indebted Poor Countries.
2. Comprehensive Development Framework pilot country.
3. Because of sustainable external debt position, it did not seek debt relief under the HIPC Initiative.
Source: Bank-Fund staff.

Table 2 Wage Bill in Selected Countries, 1999

| | Civilian Central Government | | Civilian Central Government and Armed Forces | |
	Wage bill as a percent of GDP	Wage bill as a percent of expenditures	Wage bill as a percent of GDP	Wage bill as a percent of expenditures
Benin	...	...	4.5	26.9
Bolivia	...	...	8.9	35.4
Cambodia	1.7	10.5	4.6	28.4
Macedonia, FYR	...	...	9.1	39.0
Mali	...	...	4.1	15.6
Mongolia[1]	...	...	3.3	9.3
Pakistan	0.8	3.3	...	...
Russian Federation	1.5	8.6	2.6	14.5
Tanzania[2]	...	...	3.6	24.4
Yemen, Rep. of	7.6	26.1	11.5	39.3
Zambia[3]	4.1	14.2	5.4	18.3

... = not available.

1. IMF staff, 2000.

2. Includes local governments. This is equivalent to the general government wage bill.

3. Staff estimates of wage adjustment are included, allocated according to the ratio of defense to nondefense personnel.

priority areas. Additional pressures on spending have also arisen from growing pension liabilities in some countries (Benin, Mali, Pakistan, Tanzania, the Republic of Yemen, and Zambia). In particular, sustainability of pension systems has been affected by: (a) insufficient contributions; (b) lack of a clear distinction between social insurance and social assistance roles of the schemes; (c) overly generous benefit formulas; and (d) worsening demographics.

Even when the wage bill per se is not a major risk (such as in Cambodia, Mali, Pakistan, and Russia) the use of multiple allowances that are not captured by the wage bill can still add to budget pressures, and the structural questions about the efficiency of government in these countries remain.

The size of government employment has a direct impact on the wage bill and therefore influences the overall fiscal balance. Table 3 shows that civilian central government employment varies across the 11 countries — from 0.2 percent of total population to 1.4 percent of total population. Efforts to downsize the civil service have met with limited success because of: (a) insufficient efforts to redefine the role of government and to better organize the structure of government administration; (b) a

Table 3 Public Employment in Selected Countries, 1996–99 (percent of total population)

	Benin	Bolivia	Cambodia	Macedonia, FYR	Mali	Mongolia	Pakistan	Russia	Tanzania	Yemen, Rep. of	Zambia
Total Public Employment	...	2.8	...	...	...	...	2.3	...	1.4	...	...
o/w: General Government	...	2.7	3.4	...	0.4	5.6	2.0	4.4	1.0	3.5	1.3
o/w: Civilian Central Government and Armed Forces[1]	0.3	0.5	1.7	1.7	...	2.0	0.7	1.1	0.5	2.6	0.5
o/w: Civilian Central Government[1]	0.2	0.3	0.5	1.4	...	1.2	0.3	0.4	0.4	1.2	0.2
o/w: Education[2]	0.3	1.3	0.7	1.6	...	1.9	0.7	1.5	0.4	0.7	0.5
o/w: Health[2]	0.1	0.2	0.2	1.1	...	1.1	0.2	1.3	0.1	0.1	0.2

Note: o/w means "of which." This convention is used here to convey that the indented categories of employment are subsets of the preceding categories, but are not necessarily mutually exclusive. For example, although Health, Education, and Civilian Central Government and Armed Forces are each subsets of General Government, they cannot be summed to arrive at the number for General Government.

1. Excludes education, health, and police, if available.

2. Comprises employees of central and subnational government, where applicable.

Source: World Bank and IMF staff papers.

growing trend to devolve responsibilities to subnational governments; (c) an inability to resist pressures to provide government employment (the Republic of Yemen); (d) political patronage (Bolivia, Cambodia, and Mongolia); and (e) difficulty in changing wage and employment practices due to the presence of strong labor unions (Benin, Bolivia, and Zambia).

Structural Concerns in the Country Cases

With respect to structural concerns, the country cases provided in Annex 2 employ a standard classification to ensure comparability, but the organizational structures and employment categories within government often defy simple typologies and raise particular challenges in determining the aggregate wage bill and employment. Distinguishing between core civil service and social sector employment, and between federal and central government and subnational government, is key.[6]

Wage levels continue to pose a difficult problem for many governments, caught between the political pressures to compress pay—offering comparatively generous salaries at lower levels—and the loss of their senior staff to the private sector. Chronic shortages of qualified labor in certain areas present particular challenges. Among the 11 country studies, low and compressed wage levels have led to difficulties in hiring and retaining qualified staff, particularly at the senior level in Bolivia, Cambodia, the FYR of Macedonia, Mali, Russia, the Republic of Yemen, and Zambia. However, the evidence suggests that average government wages are not low relative to per capita GDP, which merely highlights the complexity of the issue.[7] Furthermore, pay policy is frequently obscured by multiple and often opaque allowances (Benin, Mongolia, Zambia, Pakistan, and Russia). Some groups of staff can be overpaid in comparison with the private sector, while others with scarce skills are underpaid. The Macedonian case identifies overstaffing in the health and education sectors, and the Tanzanian case highlights the excess of teachers in urban centers.

Lack of accountability and poor service delivery are noted as major concerns. These lead to a focus on petty corruption, moonlighting, and "daylighting," although their association with low pay is unclear. The absence of a professional, merit-based civil service, and distorted incentive systems that discourage competent staff from remaining in the civil service were raised more often than any other issue in the country case studies. In particular, the weak link between performance and advancement is identified as an issue in Benin, Pakistan, Russia, and the Republic of Yemen; and the absence of a clear career path is a significant concern in Bolivia and Cambodia. In some countries (Cambodia, Mali, the

Republic of Yemen, and Zambia) the need for civil service reform programs to combat administrative corruption and to improve service delivery in key sectors is emphasized. Many of the cases refer to patronage in recruitment and appointments, and to corruption and its impact on service users. The cases note the link between political patronage, high turnover following elections, and a weak public service ethos in Bolivia and Mongolia.

III

Civil Service Reforms in Bank- and Fund-Supported Programs

Both the Bank and the Fund have included various dimensions of civil service reform in the programs they support. The immediate objectives of Bank-Fund involvement have been to:

- Ensure that the wage bill and the pension system are consistent with a sustainable fiscal framework.

- Streamline pay and career structures (with wage levels linked to appropriate private sector comparators), address shortages of qualified labor, and enhance incentives for senior staff performance.

- Improve accountability and service delivery (particularly in health and education), reduce corruption and partisan influence, and provide assistance to restructure key functions such as tax administration.

Prior to the introduction of adjustment lending, the World Bank was not substantially involved with civil service reforms. This changed in the early 1980s when the Bank became more engaged with administrative and civil service reforms in the context of broader public sector and governance reforms. Civil service reforms are now a fundamental part of the Bank's agenda to reduce poverty. In addition, the Bank supports the introduction of coordination mechanisms within government that provide a clear focal point for sustaining reform programs. The Fund's increased focus, since the 1980s, on fiscal and structural problems has also resulted in more attention being paid to civil service reform. This is likely to continue, although the focus would be on those elements with significant macroeconomic impact.

Fund-Supported Programs

Civil service reform becomes a part of Fund-supported programs to the extent that it is required to ensure macroeconomic stability and sustainability. Although 60 percent of all Fund-supported programs in 2000 contained elements of civil service reform, only 30 percent of these included specific performance criteria or benchmarks. More than 40 percent of Poverty Reduction Growth Facility (PRGF)[8] programs included specific benchmarks or performance criteria, while in the case of Extended Fund Facilities (EFFs),[9] only one in eight included specific conditionality (see Annex 1).

Benchmarks in recent Fund-supported programs have included annual downsizing of civil service employment within a medium-term strategy (Cambodia and Zambia). Other programs have called for: (a) rationalization, retrenchment, and initiation of pay reform (Tanzania and the FYR of Macedonia); and (b) establishment of a committee to formulate a medium-term wage policy aimed at the gradual reduction in the wage bill (the Republic of Yemen).

Fund-supported programs also have recognized that structural reforms in the civil service are often critical for fiscal sustainability. In particular, issues related to the size of the wage bill frequently can be resolved only by addressing the payroll system,[10] the size and structure of the work force (including conditions for retirement), and the nature of the pension system. In this regard, Fund conditionality on civil service reform in the 11 country cases has included: (a) completion of a civil service census and elimination of ghost workers (Cambodia); (b) passage of legislation on retirement and civil service packages, streamlining retirement procedures, and the retirement of 9,000 over-age civil servants (the Republic of Yemen);[11] (c) improvements in payroll systems and implementation of a performance-based compensation system (Benin); and (d) presentation of a plan to make the civil service pension system actuarially sound (Zambia).

In light of the recent discussions on streamlining conditionalities in Fund-supported programs,[12] it is noteworthy that several of the case studies make reference to an improved division of labor between the Bank and the Fund in the area of civil service reform. It is also presumed that under streamlined conditionality some elements of civil service reform now found in Fund-supported programs would be shifted to Bank-supported programs. In the Republic of Yemen, for example, while it is expected that the Fund will encourage the authorities to restrain the wage bill in the future and continue progress in civil service reform, conditionalities in these areas are expected to shift to the Bank. On the other hand, in Bolivia it is envisaged that both the Fund and the Bank will continue to monitor progress in reforming customs and the National Tax Service. Structural benchmarks for the reform of the two agencies are likely to be included in future Fund-supported programs.

Bank-Supported Programs

The World Bank seeks to facilitate reform in several ways. Some Bank operations address civil service reform directly, identifying the core civil service as the explicit object of reform. In fiscal 1999 and fiscal 2000, there were 45 operations with explicit civil service reform components, representing 9 percent of total Bank operations. In addition, the Bank supports many reforms in the health and education sectors that affect the employment arrangements for these staffs. The majority of civilian central government staff is in these sectors. Finally, the Bank is increasingly supporting decentralization and "community-driven" approaches that seek to stimulate better-quality services from central government. In fiscal 1999 and fiscal 2000, 60 percent of Bank operations had at least one public sector reform and governance component.

Most of the Bank's explicit civil service reform operations are in Africa, but the regional balance is changing. The profile of the adjustment operations[13] indicates that downsizing is undertaken only with support for accompanying structural reforms, and a rough balance exists between the three overarching reform objectives (correcting fiscal imbalances, reforming pay and career structures, and improving accountability and service delivery). The profile of investment operations[14] during fiscal 1999 and fiscal 2000 indicates that the emphasis is on accountability and service delivery, but always in tandem with other structural reforms, and that training and provision of information technology and other office equipment are rarely undertaken unless they support a larger structural reform (see Annex 1).

Conditionalities in Bank-supported programs have included: (a) reform of nonwage compensation rules (Benin); (b) specific institutional benchmarks on the restructuring of government agencies (such as the Customs and National Tax Service), entailing separate salary structures for the reformed agencies; (c) reduction in government employment and reform of pay scales (Zambia); and (d) steps to make the civil service more meritocratic and career-oriented (the FYR of Macedonia).

Bank-supported programs increasingly recognize that the political incentives for reform can be strengthened in two ways. First, programmatic adjustment operations[15] can help assure governments that long-term structural reforms will continue to receive Bank financing. Longer-term programmatic adjustment operations, including Poverty Reduction Support Credits (PRSC), have been introduced to encourage the necessary political acceptance of the short-term pain that civil service reforms often bring. However, including civil service reform as part of these longer-term operations may not allow for enough technical support and monitoring of reform measures. In this regard, parallel civil service investment loans can allow for sustained support and closer scrutiny of the implementation of reform measures.

A second way to strengthen the political incentives for reform is to encourage civil society to demand better governance by providing information on the quality of services, including through beneficiary monitoring of service delivery. Depending on the context, decentralization and other community-driven solutions to the delivery of government services can also assist. Public monitoring of progress in the implementation of reforms helps to promote sustainability. The acceptance of civil service reform is further bolstered by the publication of evidence on the impact of reform measures on improving the provision of public goods and services.

Elements of civil service reform seek to address administrative corruption. Bank reforms have included the introduction of an independent Public Service Commission that aims to ensure that recruitment and promotion in Pakistan are based on merit. A similar body is planned for the newly developed civil service in Bolivia. Some Fund-supported programs have been closely aligned with these objectives. For example, structural benchmarks for the Fund-supported program with Benin included the adoption of a law against the illegal acquisition of wealth.

IV

The Effectiveness of Bank and Fund Interventions

Civil service reforms have been only modestly successful in terms of meeting either macrofiscal or structural objectives. What has been especially problematic is the simultaneous achievement of both macrofiscal and structural objectives, since there may be tradeoffs between the two. For example, an overall reduction in real public sector wages may help to trim the wage bill but exacerbate difficulties in retaining skilled staff. In a similar way, there may be tradeoffs between different structural components of a civil service reform. For instance, introducing a higher pay scale in a ministry or department and protecting it from political interference may attract skilled staff from other public agencies. However, this will leave those other public agencies with a lower skill base, and thus lower chances of effective service delivery.

Whether for these reasons or others, capping, or reducing the wage bill has often proved to be unsustainable in the medium term. However, the picture is difficult to read, because central government employment has been falling globally in both reforming and nonreforming countries alike.[16] Thus, the contribution of individual Bank- or Fund-supported programs and the effectiveness of reforms, including design of social safety nets, must be distinguished from this underlying trend.

On the structural side, it is striking that, despite the intensity of reform programs in Africa, real wages have continued to show a significant decline. Reviews of effectiveness may paint a less than rosy picture of individual interventions, but they have generated some insights that seem to be influencing current reforms. The importance of understanding the pattern of total compensation, including complex interactions between allowances, has become clearer. Similarly, the greater attention paid to corruption has shown that there are few simplistic linkages with levels of pay. More generally, there is ample evidence that large-scale introduction of fixed-term contracts and performance-based pay is unlikely to be feasible or productive.

Why Has Success Been Limited?

Transformation of the civil service is one of the most politically sensitive and difficult government reforms. As a result, it is not surprising that the track record of civil service reform is modest for both institutions. Still, there are several additional reasons why progress has been limited:

- **The reform objectives have at times been unfocused, and occasionally contradictory.** Figure 1 (on page 4) outlines the typical objectives of civil service reform programs. Bank- and Fund-supported programs often include multiple objectives in civil service reform, which have occasionally been contradictory, and often not made explicit. In addition, there has been little consensus on what constitutes an acceptable approach to addressing each objective.

- **Reform programs have paid too little attention to political or other institutional constraints.** Stakeholders have different perceptions about the benefits of civil service reforms. Quite frequently these reforms are obstructed by influential vested interests that do not see any immediate advantage from the reforms. When governments provide employment as a social safety net to segments of the population, reducing public sector employment deprives them of a key policy instrument. Indeed, reducing political patronage in public sector employment may undermine the stability of the very government that must support reform. Governments also can have internally conflicting objectives, with the ministry of finance focused on fiscal savings but other ministries more concerned with salary increases. The public is often sympathetic to public servants and supportive of their demands for pay raises; but the public may accept that raises are only possible if total employment is reduced.

- **Data are rarely of sufficient quality or clarity to inform policy choices.** Weak data have prevented governments from modeling alternative scenarios or choosing between different courses of action. Along with basic aggregate wage and employment data, key data that are often missing include a sectoral breakdown of wages and employment, wage scales in different sectors, and comparisons of wage levels with those in the private sector.

V
Bank-Fund Collaboration in Civil Service Reform

The Bank and the Fund have a long history of working together on civil service reform. On occasion, structural reform measures are included in both Bank- and Fund-supported programs. In the 11 country cases such instances were found in: (a) the promotion of merit-based hiring (Benin, Bolivia, Cambodia, FYR Macedonia, Mongolia, and Russia); (b) the improvement of payroll systems (Zambia); (c) fiscal decentralization (Bolivia, Mali, Pakistan, Tanzania, and Zambia); and (d) a shift from targeting employment numbers to placing controls on the budget (Zambia).

The case studies also show that civil service reform remains on the agenda for future Bank- and Fund-supported programs. The two staffs see many areas for needed reforms. These include: (a) professionalization of the civil service (Benin, Mongolia, and Pakistan); (b) improvements in the payroll system (Cambodia, Mongolia, Pakistan, and Zambia) and pay reform (Benin, the Republic of Yemen, and Zambia); (c) reductions in the size of the wage bill (Bolivia, FYR Macedonia, Mongolia, the Republic of Yemen, and Zambia); and (d) increases in the quantity and quality of services delivered (Cambodia, Mali, Mongolia, Pakistan, and Tanzania).

The reform challenges facing the civil service—improving incentives through pay and career structures, and improving service delivery, accountability, and transparency—are largely structural issues, but they have major macrofiscal implications. Joint involvement has been productive, with selective Fund conditionality usefully supporting Bank operations and Bank conditionality usefully supporting Fund operations. Past Fund-supported programs have included conditionality on the wage bill and on the size of civil service employment, as well as on structural reforms. However, the focus on the wage bill has tended to have little impact on overall employment because of institutional and political factors. Moreover, reductions in real public sector wages may have exacerbated difficulties in retaining skilled staff.

Bank-supported programs have included conditionality on the restructuring of government agencies, reform of nonwage compensation rules, reduction in government employment, reform of pay scales, and steps to make the civil service more meritocratic and career-oriented. But even here there have been tradeoffs between different structural components of civil service reform, as well as a lack of clarity with regard to objectives.

Problems have arisen from uncoordinated actions by donors. However, conflicts between the Bank and the Fund have been infrequent. This is, in part, because the relationship between the two institutions has generally improved with early dialogue and the building of personal relationships between staff. Under streamlining, it is probable that a clearer distinction will be drawn between structural conditionalities within Bank operations and macroeconomic benchmarks and performance criteria in Fund programs.

The timing and sequencing of reforms in Bank- and Fund-supported programs have not always been made explicit. This is partly attributable to the lack of an articulated strategy for the short and medium term by the two institutions at the country level. This has made it difficult for governments to determine whether the Bank and the Fund are providing consistent advice. Timing and sequencing of macrofiscal and structural reforms in the strategies of the two institutions reflect the different time horizons of the programs that they support. In some cases, short-term macroeconomic objectives (such as the need to reduce government spending) have run counter to longer-term structural reforms (such as the need to decompress wages and improve pay structures).

While the framework of collaboration between the Bank and the Fund has been enhanced for low-income countries in the context of the Poverty Reduction Strategy Paper (PRSP) process, there has been less progress in middle-income countries. Both country groups could benefit from a more effective Bank-Fund partnership in support of country programs. The principles noted in the recently established Joint Guidelines include: clarity on primary responsibilities, full consultations between institutions, and distinct accountability in lending decisions. These principles would ensure clarity of roles, improve accountability, and increase transparency. In the area of civil service reform the staff of the two institutions will report to their Boards on the role of each institution and the responsibilities of the institution taking the lead.[17]

The overall conclusion to emerge from the September workshop is that Bank and Fund staff should engage in a dialogue earlier in the reform process, and with greater focus. Systematic and early sharing of information and institutional views is crucial. There are opportunities for early agreements within the framework of the Bank Country Assistance Strategy (CAS) and Fund Article IV consultations and program discussions. At least for low-income countries the PRSP process (particularly the Joint Staff Assessment) could provide a vehicle for coordination. Yet it is not clear whether existing PRSPs and Interim PRSPs (I-PRSPs) are adequate in terms of their specificity regarding civil service reforms.

Principles for Collaboration

Collaboration between the Bank and the Fund should rest on the following six foundations:

- **Be more selective.** Selectivity and consistency of objectives are crucial. The priority afforded to different elements of the reform agenda can and should differ among civil service reform programs. Therefore, these priorities should be defined on a country-specific basis.

- **Develop a medium-term fiscal framework.** Short-run policies aimed at protecting macroeconomic stability cannot ignore longer-run implications, and long-run structural reforms should not ignore the short-run fiscal impacts. Therefore, it is important to locate civil service reforms in the context of a medium-term framework. Such a framework would allow for the incorporation of the fiscal impact of the structural reform in civil service reform.

- **Foster national ownership by making reforms politically feasible.** A first step could involve identifying stakeholders and then discussing tradeoffs in the absence of reform. In particular, the postponement of reforms could imply continued high employment and a high tax burden for the economy, with continuing poor service provision.

- **Focus and streamline conditionality.** The recent Board paper[18] makes recommendations for a judicious approach to conditionality. The lead agency concept agreed on by both institutions should prove useful in coordinating conditionalities in Bank- and Fund-supported programs. Wage bill or employment targets in Fund-supported programs should be consistent with longer-term reforms being supported by the Bank. The Bank would take the lead in advising on structural reforms and in defining structural conditionalities. Bank staff should provide guideposts and a timeline for these reforms, and seek to quantify their fiscal impact within the aforementioned medium-term framework. This will ensure the viability and sustainability of fiscal reforms. There was also agreement that selective and judicious use of Fund conditionality may still be needed to support reforms, particularly in crisis countries.

- **Agree on sequencing and timing of reforms.** Sequencing and timing of reforms will have to be country-specific. For example, downsizing and reform of pay and grade structures is a judgment that has to be made at the country level. Explicit discussion between the Bank, the Fund, and the government on sequencing and timing of reforms should precede decisions on key actions such as civil service censuses, functional reviews, design of retrenchment programs, or monetization and consolidation of benefits.

- **Strengthen data collection.** The workshop agreed that it is important to work toward a minimum dataset, sufficient to inform a basic model for illustrating tradeoffs in the dialogue with government. In addition to up-to-date wage and employment data, Bank and Fund staff agreed to work together to identify the core set of data required to support civil service reforms. Already, the Bank is strengthening its data collection in this area. For example, the Bank has undertaken extensive surveys of civil servants over the past 18 months, funded by the World Bank–Netherlands Partnership Program (BNPP). In addition, a new global database of government employment and wages has been established with preliminary data on 185 countries.[20]

It must be recognized that civil service reform is a long-term challenge. Strengthening political incentives for reform and ensuring the sustainability of these reform efforts require long-term support by the Bank and the Fund. Acceptance of the need for reforms can be reinforced by pressure from civil society. This would require making information available on the quality of public services and publishing evidence on the impact that reforms have on improving the provision of these goods and services. In the past, the long-term nature of civil service reform was not always recognized; but the more recent focus in the Bank on longer-term programmatic operations—supplemented where necessary by shorter-term technical assistance—is now more aligned with the task at hand.

Next Steps

Moving forward, the Bank and Fund Area Departments and Regions will agree on a small set of "focus countries" for enhanced collaboration in the area of civil service reform. Focus countries will be countries where a significant stage or phase of civil service reform is planned but has not yet been fully launched. Staff of both institutions, in collaboration with government counterparts, will make explicit the assumptions guiding the Bank and the Fund in their support of civil service reform. Moreover, both staffs, in collaboration with government, will agree on the following: (a) the priority macroeconomic, structural, and governance objectives for civil service reform, placing these within a medium-term fiscal framework; (b) the establishment of lead responsibilities in the macroeconomic (Fund) and structural (Bank) areas, while ensuring that conditionalities are kept to a minimum; (c) the sequencing and timing of the reforms; and (d) a core set of wage and employment data to support civil service reforms.

The "focus countries" approach will assist in transforming the principles agreed on at the September workshop into a readily useable approach, and will test that the principles do in fact lead to more "traction" on core civil service reform issues.

Annex 1
Civil Service Reform in Fund- and Bank-Supported Programs

Fund-Supported Programs

Table A1.1 presents data on conditionality in IMF programs related to civil service reforms, as well as broader discussion of intended reforms, although these may not be subject to conditionality.

Some examples of structural benchmarks related to civil service reform in Fund-supported programs have included: (a) implementation of a performance-based compensation system, (b) design of voluntary retirement or buyout packages, or retrenchment or retraining packages for civil servants, (c) computerization of personnel records, (d) decompression of wage scales, and (e) hiring and wage freezes.

Examples of performance criteria related to civil service reform in Fund-supported programs include: (a) lowering or freezing the size of the wage bill, such as ceilings on wage bills, (b) legislation for carrying out civil service reform, and (c) making the civil service pension system actuarially sound.

Bank-Supported Programs

The Bank has two basic types of lending instruments: investment loans and adjustment loans. Investment loans have a long-term focus (5 to 10 years) and finance goods, works, and services in support of economic and social development projects in a broad range of sectors. Adjustment loans have a short-term focus (one to three years), and provide quick-disbursing assistance to countries with external financing needs, in order to support structural reforms in a sector or in the economy as a whole. They support the policy and institutional changes needed to create an environment conducive to sustained and equitable growth.

Loans can be arranged programmatically, so that a series of operations supports a medium-term government program of policy reforms and institution building.

Table A1.1 Civil Service Conditionality in Fund-Supported Programs, 2000

	PRGF[a]	EFF[b]	SBA[c]
	(number of countries)		
All Fund-supported programs	33	8	15
Civil Service measures included as benchmarks[d]	9	1	1
Civil Service measures included as performance criteria[e]	5	0	1
Discussion in program documents of reform measures not subject to conditionality:			
Restrain the wage bill	30	4	11
Retrenchment or employment freeze, or both	14	2	0
Improve efficiency of civil service	24	8	5

Note: Some countries may have civil service reform (CSR) initiatives both as benchmarks and as performance criteria.

a. The PRGF provides medium-term assistance to countries where poverty reduction is the cornerstone of the growth-oriented economic strategy, based on a comprehensive, nationally owned PRSP prepared by the borrowing country and endorsed in their respective areas of responsibility by the Boards of the Fund and Bank as the basis for the institutions' concessional loans and for relief under the enhanced HIPC Initiative.

b. The EFF provides medium-term assistance to members with (a) an economy suffering a serious payments imbalance relating to structural maladjustments in production and trade and where price and cost distortions have been widespread; or (b) an economy characterized by slow growth and an inherently weak balance of payments position that prevents pursuit of an active development policy. The length of an EFF arrangement is typically three years and disbursement is conditional on the borrower meeting specified performance requirements, including structural reforms.

c. SBAs (stand-by arrangements) are designed to deal with any temporary balance of payments problem. The typical SBA is for 12–18 months, but may be as long as three years where disbursement of financing is usually conditional on the borrower meeting specified performance requirements.

d. Benchmarks are a point of reference against which Fund program implementation is monitored. Benchmarks are not necessarily quantitative and frequently relate to structural variables and policies.

e. Performance criteria are macroeconomic indicators (such as monetary and budgetary targets) that must be met for the member to qualify for purchases under SBA, EFF, and PRGF arrangements.

Source: IMF staff.

Some Bank operations address civil service reform directly, identifying the core civil service as the explicit object of reform.[21] In fiscal 1999 and 2000 there were 45 operations with explicit civil service reform components, representing around 9 percent of total Bank operations (see Table A1.2). This dramatically understates the level of Bank activity in

Table A1.2 Civil Service Interventions in Bank Operations (operations approved in fiscal 1999 and fiscal 2000)

	Programmatic	Nonprogrammatic
Investment	6[a]	27[b]
Adjustment	2[c]	10[d]

a. APLs; b. Specific investment loans; sector investment and maintenance loans; learning and innovation loans; and technical assistance loans; c. Programmatic structural adjustment loans and PRSC; d. Structural and sector adjustment loans; special structural adjustment loans; structural adjustment loans.
Source: Bank staff.

reforming public employment arrangements, however. The Bank supports many health- and education-sector reforms that affect the employment arrangements for these staffs and the majority of civilian central government staff that are in these sectors. The Bank is also increasingly supporting decentralization and "community-driven" approaches that seek to stimulate better quality services from central government. In fiscal 1999 and fiscal 2000, 60 percent of Bank operations had at least one public sector reform and governance component.

Adjustment operations have an impact on government policy by requiring that significant policy actions are taken either prior to approval of the loan or as a condition of subsequent tranche releases. In core civil service reforms the required policy changes can typically be seen in five areas. Table A1.3 indicates how many of the 12 adjustment operations in fiscal 1999 and fiscal 2000 included a component targeting one of these specific reforms.

In addition, conditionalities under adjustment lending addressed reform coordination mechanisms within government in 4 of the 12 operations.

A detailed examination of the profile of adjustment operations during this two-year period indicates that downsizing is not undertaken without support for accompanying structural reforms, and that there is a broad balance between the three overarching reform objectives (correcting fiscal imbalances, reforming pay and career structures, and improving accountability and service delivery).

Investment operations generally focus on more specific interventions. Table A1.4 summarizes the interventions supported by investment operations, with the figures in parentheses indicating the number of operations that addressed these particular issues out of the 33 investment

Table A1.3 Policy Reforms in World Bank Adjustment Operations (operations approved in fiscal 1999 and fiscal 2000)

Correct fiscal imbalances	Pay and career structures	Improving accountability and service delivery
Downsizing (such as hiring freezes and attrition, abolition of vacant posts, early retirement, voluntary severance, removal of tenure, compulsory redundancies, and caps on the aggregate wage bill) [6/12]	Revised pay and grading [6/12]	Strengthening user voice (such as surveys, administrative law reform) [4/12] Strengthening merit (such as independent oversight of recruitment, updating or introducing job descriptions, updating or introducing performance appraisal, senior executive service) [4/12] Organizational restructuring and accountability improvements (such as functional reviews, governance of newly created agencies, agency performance reports) [6/12]

Table A1.4 Interventions Supported by World Bank Investment Operations (operations approved in fiscal 1999 and fiscal 2000)

Correct fiscal imbalances	Pay and career structures	Improving accountability and service delivery
Civil service censuses [6/33] Creating redeployment funds [2/33]	Job reclassification [7/33] HR training [9/33] Improving payroll management and introducing human resources management information systems [10/33] Selective salary enhancements [2/33]	Management training [26/33] Information technology (IT) and office equipment [20/33] Improving appraisal systems [11/33] Competitive performance improvement/challenge funds [4/33] Restructuring and reengineering organizations [14/33]

operations that focused on core civil service reforms in fiscal 1999 and fiscal 2000.

The profile of investment operations during fiscal 1999 and fiscal 2000 indicates that the emphasis is on accountability and service delivery—though always in tandem with other structural reforms—and that training and provision of IT and other office equipment are rarely undertaken unless they support a larger structural reform.

Annex 2
Country Notes

Benin

1. Size and Structure of Civilian Central Government

Benin's Civilian Central Government (excluding education, health, and police) is organized into a career structure with five employment grades, each divided into multiple levels. Within grades employees ascend automatically after two years at each level. Once at the top of an employment grade, a promotion is required to move to the next grade. The number of promotions is limited by predetermined percentages (from 40 percent to 10 percent for the intermediary to the outstanding grade).

By moving up one level, a civil servant typically receives a double-digit salary increase. The system of nonwage benefits can increase base salary by as much as 50 percent.

2. Key Institutional and Structural Concerns

Among the institutional concerns confronting Benin's civil service are the following:

- **Promotion.** Advancement has not been tied to performance. (Although promotions have been scarce due to budgetary constraints, within a grade a civil servant can expect to climb all the steps of the ladder over a 24-year career and get a salary increase at each step.) Appointments to management positions are frequently based on political ties.

- **Weak personnel management system.** There is little communication between the general personnel management system and ministries, or between the civil service roster and the payroll system. In 1997 the Ministry of the Civil Service (MoCS) conducted a physical census of civil service. The MoCS is still updating its files based on the results

Figure 2A.1   The Main Components of Government Employment in Benin, circa 1998

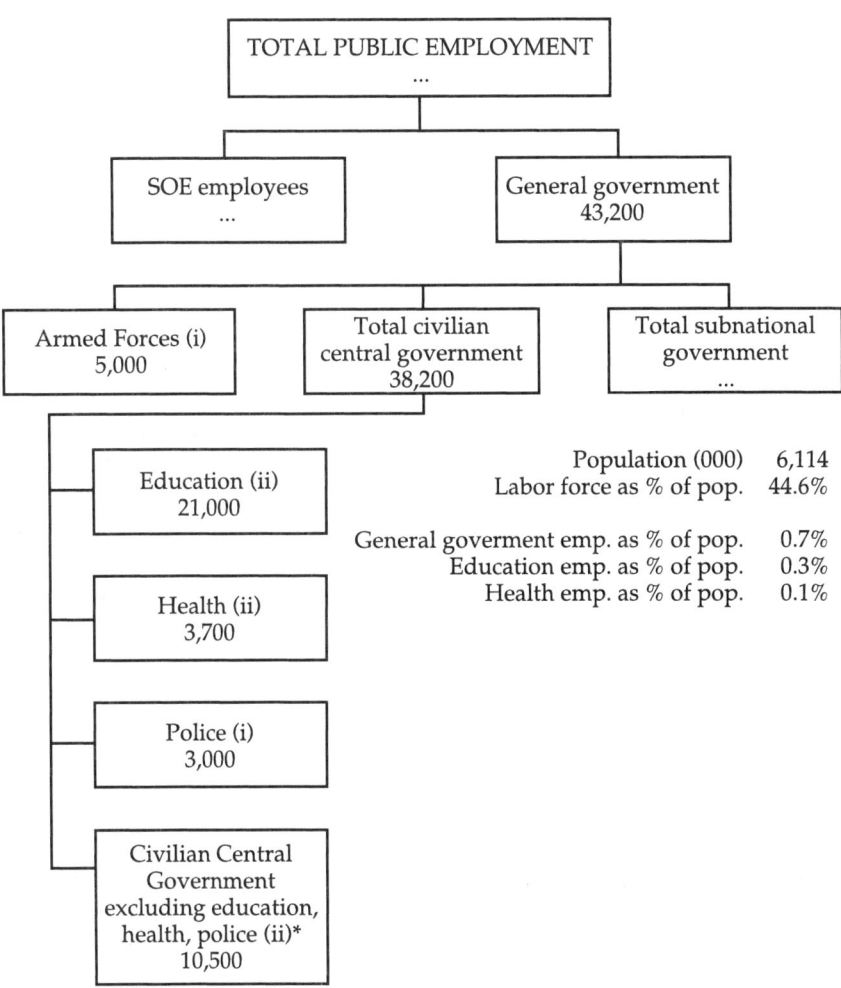

Sources and dates covered: (i) Updated WB database on PS employment—1996–99; gendarmerie are classified as police. (ii) Benin Ministry of the Civil Service; education figure includes approximately 4,000 contract employees, and the health figure includes approximately 1,000. If no source is shown, then the total is calculated arithmetically. *Diplomats are also excluded.

from 1997. In 1999 the Ministry of Finance (MoF) decided to conduct yet another civil service census to update their files for the payroll. Absenteeism is rife.

• **Retirement rules.** The retirement age is 55, but those who have served for 30 years before reaching age 55 may also retire. In March 2001 about 79 percent of civil servants were at least 40 years old.

• **Mismatch between actual and grade-based salaries.** From 1986 to 1992 civil service wages were frozen, but advancements continued within the career structure, creating a gap between position and pay. General salary increases have been granted since 1992, but the gap between actual salary payments and grade-based salaries was never fully closed.

3. Recent and Current Institutional Reforms

Many bilateral and multilateral institutions have supported public administration reform in Benin, contributing an estimated US$50 million over the period 1990–98. There has been little to show for these efforts.

Preparation of a new pay scale (see Table A2.1) and a performance-based compensation mechanism was completed with Bank assistance in early 1998. A law introducing the reform was adopted by the National Assembly in September 1998. It would reform nonwage compensation rules, gradually eliminate the discrepancies between actual salary payments and grade-based salaries over a period of four years, and create a new pay scale with performance-based compensation features. By continuing the policy of hiring two civil servants for every three retirees, it was estimated that the increase in the wage bill would be limited to 5 percent a year. However, implementation of this reform is still waiting for the National Assembly to amend the law on the compensation system, as required by the Constitutional Court.

Table A2.1 Benin Average Wages, 1997

	Nominal LCU[a]	Ratio of average wage to per capita GDP
Average Government Wage	1,648,000	7.6

a. LCU is local currency unit.
Source: Updated WB database on PS employment: 1996–99.

Enacting civil service reform has proved extremely difficult, due in part to the close interrelation between trade union leaders, public officials (themselves union members), and the parliament, where civil servants represent the majority of deputies.[22] All public employees are unionized, and the unions have demanded pay increases to make up for an earlier wage freeze (see below) as the starting point for any discussion of reform. The current Minister of Civil Service, Employment, and Administrative Reform is himself a former union leader.

4. Key Macrofiscal Concerns

Measures to contain the wage bill in Benin have included (a) a voluntary departure scheme, which led to more than 6,000 departures during 1990–96; (b) a wage freeze from 1986 to 1992; and (c) an attrition policy that allows only two replacements for every three departures. The wage bill fell from 7.2 percent of GDP to 4.6 percent over the same period, and from 107 percent of tax revenue to 34 percent. This reduction in the relative size of the wage bill was produced, in part, by declining real wages following the devaluation of the CFA franc in January 1994 (see Table A2.2).

Existing staffing needs, the elimination of discrepancies between actual salary payments and grade-based salaries, and the decentralization process will put pressure on the wage bill and could jeopardize macroeconomic stability. Given the unmet personnel requirements in health

Table A2.2 Benin: The Main Dimensions of the Public Sector Wage Bill (all units are local currency, 1999)

	Nominal LCU	Percent of GDP	Percent of government expenditure
Total Civilian Central Government and Armed Forces Wage Bill (millions)	66,300	4.5	26.9
Memo items:			
GDP (millions)	1,463,300		
GDP per capita	239,334		
Total central government expenditure (millions):	246,300		

Sources: Statistical Appendix, IMF 2000; and WB *World Development Indicators* database.

and education, total employment in the central government is expected to increase. In addition, it is estimated that reestablishing salaries at grade level would increase the wage bill by one-third (about 1.5 percent of GDP). The authorities have agreed to grant a gradual catch-up as a counterpart for moving to the new pay scale and performance-based compensation, and are designing methods to prevent the decentralization process from weakening fiscal policy and expenditure control.

The deficit of the Fonds National de Retraite du Bénin (Civil Service Pension Fund, FNRB) is covered by the budget, amounting to 0.5 percent of GDP, and is rising continuously, reflecting the rapidly rising number of civil servants reaching retirement age and the decline in the number of contributing civil servants.

5. Need for Including Civil Service Reforms in PRSC and PRGF Programs?

Improving the efficiency of the civil service and maintaining a stable macroeconomic framework will require including civil service reforms in PRGF-supported programs. The PRGF program should focus primarily on the fiscal implications of the planned reforms, while the Bank and other creditors would focus on the technical work regarding the new pay scale and performance-based promotion mechanism.

6. Benchmarks for the Future. How Will Progress be Monitored?

The implementation of a new pay scale and performance-based compensation mechanism is critical for containing the wage bill (by eliminating automatic step increases and their corresponding pay increases). Benchmarks in this area should consist of specific measures to indicate full implementation, as well as medium-term overall fiscal objectives.

Bolivia

1. Size and Structure of Civilian Central Government

Figure A2.2 The Main Components of Government Employment in Bolivia, 1999

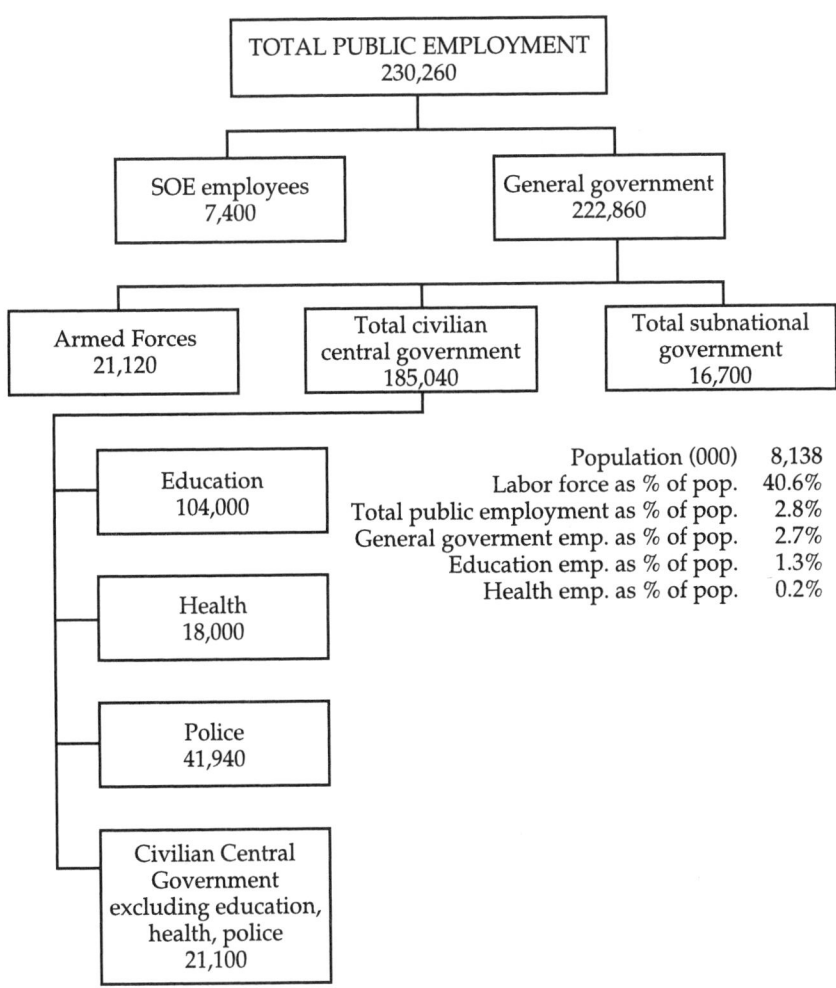

Source: Republic of Bolivia, Office of the Vice President, 1999.

2. Key Institutional and Structural Concerns

Public staff recruitment in Bolivia is based on political patronage. Party loyalty is rewarded with public jobs, and it is common for the parties in power to finance themselves by deducting contributions from their public employees' wages. This mechanism creates incentives for the authorities to raise the wage bill in order to maximize the amount of resources available for political use, and has increased the level of public liabilities substantially, particularly at the municipal level. The government's hiring procedures also generate high turnover rates, since the mobility of high-level public officials entails the reallocation of loyal employees. The high turnover has prevented the development of a public service ethic, and adversely affects the efficiency and quality of the government's services.

3. Recent and Current Institutional Reforms

Various reform programs have aimed at restricting the problem by issuing regulations that encourage transparent hiring procedures, based only on the employee's professional qualifications. There have also been attempts to rationalize the wage bill in the health and education sectors. However, the reforms have been unsuccessful because the concentration of political power, including that of the health and education workers' unions, remains untouched. Major structural reforms—including an end to political party financing out of civil service wages, judicial modernization, and further decentralization—should be undertaken to help limit the arbitrary use of power, limit the power of unions, and achieve greater transparency and efficiency in hiring procedures and in determining the appropriate size and composition of the civil service.

A comprehensive attempt at civil reform is embodied in Bolivia's Civil Service Statute of 1999. The Act provided for (a) establishment of an independent civil service superintendent's office as an overseer of government-wide personnel management; (b) introduction of merit-based

Table A2.3. Bolivia: Average Wages, 1999

	Nominal LCU[a]	Ratio of average wage to per capita GDP
Average Government Wage	20,921	3.5

a. LCU is local currency unit.
Source: Calculated from data in Figure A2.2 and Table A2.4.

recruitment processes; (c) a management-by-results bureaucracy to increase efficiency, transparency, and accountability; and (d) decentralizing government functions.

Currently, the Bolivian government is working to reform the structure, organization, and operational processes of targeted public agencies on an agency-by-agency basis. This will imply a separate salary structure for reformed agencies. In each case, the salary structure is defined by balancing fiscal prudence and the need to offer competitive salaries. The process is monitored through quantitative and verifiable targets, including International Standards Organization (ISO) certification.

The reform is facing delays. Some political elites feel threatened by the introduction of merit principles that a successful reform would produce. However, isolated successes—the product of a few tenacious young technocrats—can be observed, such as the institutionalization of the Customs Administration. Since the media and civil society favor the civil service reform, politicians could leverage this support.

4. Key Macrofiscal Concerns

While much of Bolivia's civil service reform focuses on improving governance, the agency-specific reforms in the National Tax Service and the Customs Administration will have a macroeconomic impact, as well, by enhancing the government's ability to collect taxes. Both elements are critical for the authorities to raise tax revenues by 4 percentage points of GDP by 2007, as projected in the PRSP. The civil service reform should also help to underpin the medium-term goal of fiscal sustainability (the PRSP framework proposes growth of the wage bill in line with expected inflation — see Table A2.4).

The Fund has contributed to the reform of the Customs Administration (taking the lead as a coordinator) and of the National Tax Service (by developing a framework for the reform).

5. Need for Including Civil Service Reforms in PRSC and PRGF Programs?

The reforms of the customs and domestic tax administrations are important for the PRGF-supported program and should be monitored. Bank staff will need to weigh the merits of linking the civil service reform to a PRSC rather than an adaptable program loan (APL). The PRSC might be a better instrument if the fiduciary framework (including financial systems and procurement) is deemed sufficiently strong, while the APL permits closer supervision and better technical assistance. The most important advantage of a PRSC is, potentially, greater leverage, with the coordination of donor assistance around a single agreed on program.

Table A2.4 Bolivia: The Main Dimensions of the Public Sector Wage Bill (all units are local currency, 1999)

	Nominal LCU[a]	Percent of GDP	Percent of government expenditure
Total Civilian Central Government and Armed Forces Wage Bill (millions)	4,313	8.9	35.4
Memo items:			
GDP (millions)	48,605		
GDP per capita	5,973		
Total central government expenditure (millions)	12,179		

a. LCU is local currency unit.
Sources: Statistical Appendix, IMF June 21, 2001; and WB *World Development Indicators* database.

6. Benchmarks for the Future.
How Will Progress Be Monitored?

Fund and Bank staffs collaborate closely in monitoring progress with the customs and National Tax Service reforms, including joint supervision missions. These reforms are integrated with the overall civil service reform. Structural benchmarks for the reform of these two agencies may continue to be included in PRGF arrangements. Policy conditionality in the Bank's APL includes five targets related to the overall civil service reform, and the Bank also monitors specific institutional benchmarks for each agency under the reform process.

Cambodia

1. Size and Structure of Civilian Central Government

Cambodia's public administration has five levels (national, provincial, district, commune, and village). However, administrative management is highly centralized. The Prime Minister appoints provincial governors, who receive almost their entire budgets from the central government and have little authority to raise revenues. To date, no subnational government has been elected. (Commune elections are scheduled for February 2002.)

2. Key Institutional and Structural Concerns

The current civil administration suffers from a number of problems including: (a) prevalence of nepotism and cronyism as a result of the lack of a competitive recruitment system; (b) widespread absenteeism and "brain-drain" due to below-subsistence, noncompetitive remuneration (average pay for civil servants was US$23 per month, far below the minimum wage of US$45 per month in the garment industry—see Table A2.5); and (c) the lack of a clear career path that could motivate staff to carry out assigned tasks.

Skilled civil servants at senior management levels (age cohorts of 40s and 50s) are in severe shortage. This reflects a mass destruction of human resources during the Khmer Rouge period (1975–79) and the lack of relevant training opportunities during the 1980s. Teachers' salary levels need to be increased significantly to attract enough staff to meet the growing need for primary and lower secondary education.

3. Recent and Current Institutional Reforms

The government is currently finalizing the medium-term civil service reform strategy with technical assistance from the Bank, the Fund, the United Nations Development Programme (UNDP), and the Asian Development Bank (AsDB). The current reform scenario for 2002–06 envisages: (a) salary decompression to allow more adequate compensation for higher-level civil servants (and so-called priority mission groups); (b) self-financing of the wage bill; and (c) increasing the number of teachers and decreasing the number of noneducation employees. Reorganization of the ministerial structure is also planned in the second phase.

Figure A2.3 The Main Components of Government Employment in Cambodia, circa 1999

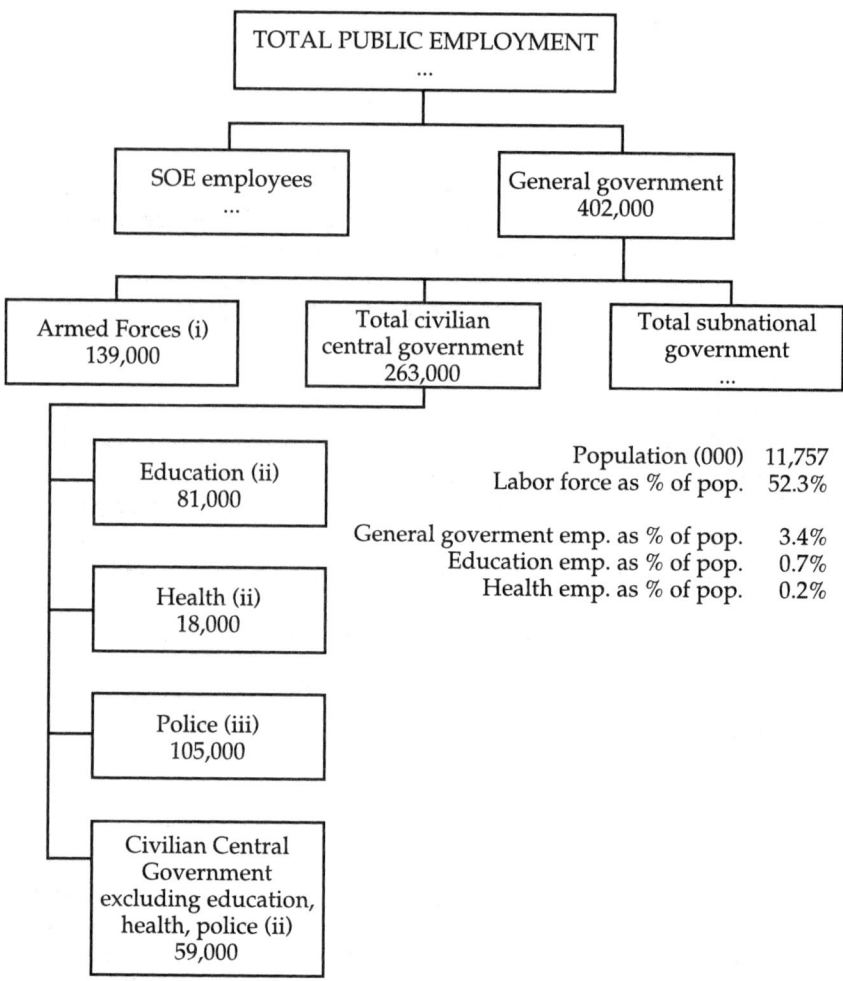

Sources and dates covered: (i) Updated WB database on PS employment—1996–99; refers to 1999; (ii) Civil service census, October 2000; (iii) this figure is for 1998, courtesy of Toshi Kato. If no source shown, then the total is calculated arithmetically.

Table A2.5 Cambodia: Average Wages, 1999

	Nominal LCU[a]	Ratio of average wage to per capita GDP
Average Government Wage	1,306,965	1.3

a. LCU is local currency unit.
Source: Calculated from data in Figure A2.3 and Table A2.6.

The first commune elections scheduled in February 2002 could potentially bring a fundamental change in the way public services are delivered for local people. The ongoing civil service reform initiative launched in 1999 is being carried out in a much less fragile political environment than during earlier efforts in 1993–97. The completion of a comprehensive civil service census—including fingerprinting and identity cards—will provide a better foundation than has existed in the past for monitoring the implementation of reforms.

The AsDB assisted in the design of Priority Mission Groups (PMGs). Bank and Fund staffs expressed reservations about the long-term impact of PMGs. The PMGs will operate outside the normal civil service pay and employment structure. Thousands of non-PMG officials would receive lower salaries than their counterparts in PMG posts. This will likely be a source of friction. Moreover, introducing PMGs might postpone reform of the core civil service structure. A medium-term integration strategy is needed to avoid the possibility of permanent, parallel civil service structures, with PMGs leaving the civil service upon completion of their appointments.

4. Key Macrofiscal Concerns

The size of Cambodia's wage bill, as a percent of GDP or total current expenditure, is not excessive in comparison to similar low-income countries. This situation, however, largely reflects unsustainably low salary levels (see above). Civil service employment in relation to total labor force or total population has been kept broadly constant, and this is projected to continue in the medium term, with a marked increase in the education sector (16 percent) partly offset by a decline (–18 percent) in other sectors. Increases in government wages over the medium term will remain directly tied to meeting revenue targets and timely implementation of military demobilization. The Bank, as well as bilateral donors, is committed to support demobilization, which should generate payroll savings. As a result, the civilian wage bill should remain below 40 percent of current expenditures (see Table A2.6).

Table A2.6 Cambodia: The Main Dimensions of the Public Sector Wage Bill (all units are local currency, 1999)

	Nominal LCU[a]	Percent of GDP	Percent of government expenditure
Total Civilian Central Government Wage Bill (millions)	194,000	1.7	10.5
Armed Forces (defense and security) Wage Bill (millions)	331,000	2.9	17.9
Total Civilian Central Gov't. and Armed Forces Wage Bill (millions)	525,400	4.6	28.4
Memo items:			
GDP (millions)	11,470,000		
GDP per capita	1,033,802		
Total central government expenditure (millions)	1,847,000		

a. LCU is local currency unit.
Sources: IMF RED tables; and WB *World Development Indicators* database for population.

A broad spectrum of international financial institution (IFI) assistance to macrofiscal reform is covered by the Fund under a three-year Technical Cooperation Action Plan (TCAP) initiated in early 2001 and by the Bank through an Economic Capacity Building project and grant assistance.

5. Need for Including Civil Service Reforms in PRSC and PRGF Programs?

A PRSC is currently envisaged for fiscal 2003, and it should include civil service reform. Both the government and the donor community agree that public sector reform is central to lay the foundations for poverty reduction and sustainable development. In particular, improving the performance of service delivery in the key sectors (health, education, agriculture, and rural development) will have a direct impact on poverty reduction in rural areas, where a majority of Cambodia's poor live.

Civil service reform has been a key component of the reform agenda since the inception of the current PRGF-supported program in October 1999. The authorities and Fund staff considered that civil service reform, in tandem with military demobilization, was central for ensuring the medium-term viability of the fiscal program and improving the delivery of public services. A division of labor between the Bank and the Fund was agreed on, whereby the Fund would monitor the overall wage bill in the context of the fiscal constraints, and the Bank would take the lead role in the design of the reform strategy.

6. Benchmarks for the Future.
How Will Progress Be Monitored?

Under the PRGF-supported program the overall wage bill is set annually in consultation with Fund staff. The overall civilian wage bill will be kept below a maximum of 40 percent of current expenditure. Annual employment levels will be contained within the parameters set under the government's medium-term strategy for civil service reform, to be implemented starting in 2002.

Cambodia recently developed a Governance Action Plan (GAP), a compendium of priority reform actions in key reform areas—the legal and judicial sector, civil administration, decentralization and local governance, public finance, anticorruption, gender equity, military reform and demobilization, and natural resources management. The government is in the process of developing benchmarks and progress indicators in collaboration with donors and civil society organizations.

Former Yugoslav Republic of Macedonia

1. Size and Structure of Civilian Central Government

The FYR of Macedonia's civilian central government stood at 4.5 percent of the population in 1998 (see Figure A2.4). This places the country in the bottom third of a set of Central and Eastern European comparator countries (Albania, Bulgaria, Croatia, the Czech Republic, Estonia, Hungary, Latvia, Lithuania, Poland, the Slovak Republic, and Turkey). However, FYR Macedonia outstrips other Central and Eastern European countries in terms of general government wage expenditures relative to both total expenditures and GDP. The General Government Wage Bill is significantly underestimated because many of the line ministries supplement wage payments from their special revenue funds, which are not recorded in either the central or general government accounts. For example, the accounting of the health fund (the largest off-budget agency) does not identify the wage bill for health staff. Off-budget entities are not generally included in these totals, but FYR Macedonia is unusual in that a large number of public sector staff are employed through such bodies.

2. Key Institutional and Structural Concerns

The salary structure does not motivate. Pay levels in the administration are severely compressed. Professional staff face weak financial incentives to take on senior positions that carry greater responsibilities and require more advanced skills. Estimates from individual ministries indicate that an undersecretary (one of the most senior posts) might earn roughly 2 to 3 times more (net, including allowances) than the lowest-paid employee such as a cleaner. This compression ratio is more extreme than those found in some other post-communist countries. Compression ratios in this range do not promise much in the way of financial benefits from an extended career in FYR Macedonia's public administration. However, decompressing the salary structure without rationalizing the size of the civil service could pose difficulties in fiscal sustainability given the size of the wage bill relative to GDP and to total spending.

Interpreting the adequacy of total compensation is difficult. Determination of actual wage levels is complicated by general problems in data availability and the decentralized wage-setting approach. Due to weaknesses at the center of government (and particularly in the MoF), wage increases have been granted in selected ministries. For example, the Ministry of Interior received an across-the-board increase of 20 percent during the spring 1999 crisis in neighboring Kosovo. Ministry of

Figure A2.4 The Main Components of Government Employment in FYR Macedonia, 1999

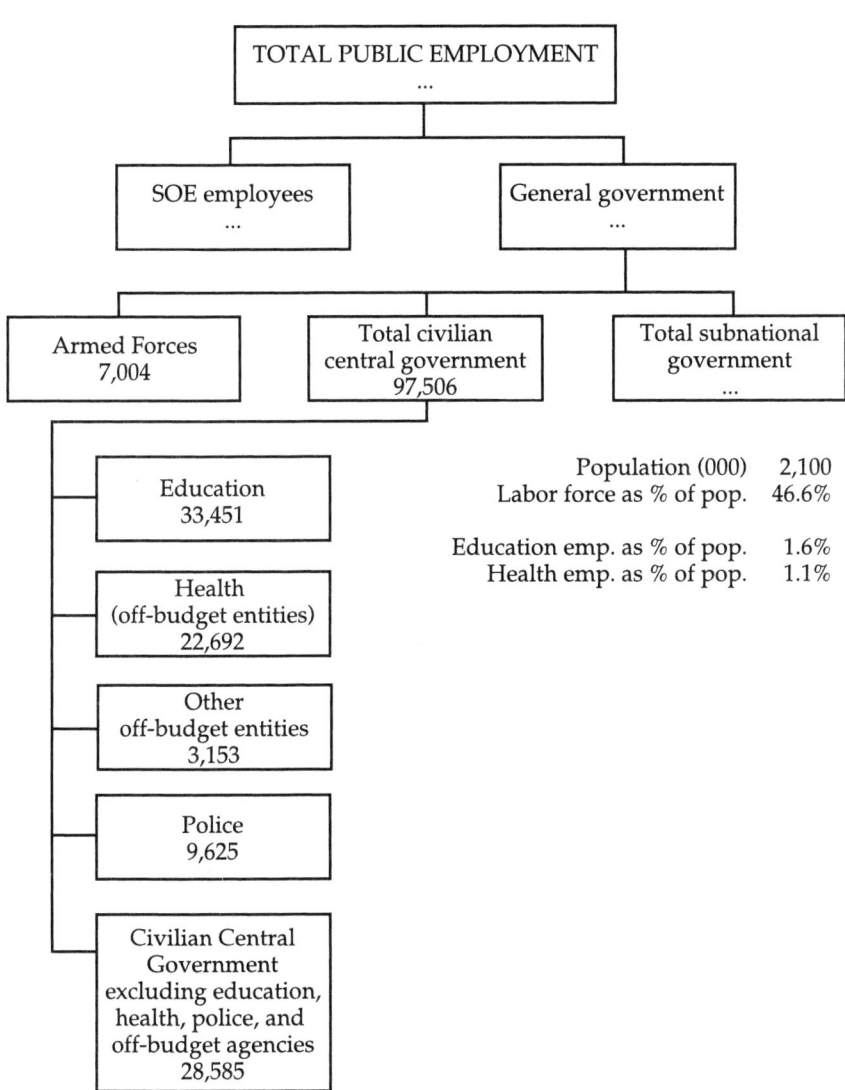

TOTAL PUBLIC EMPLOYMENT
...

SOE employees
...

General government
...

Armed Forces
7,004

Total civilian
central government
97,506

Total subnational
government
...

Education
33,451

Health
(off-budget entities)
22,692

Other
off-budget entities
3,153

Police
9,625

Civilian Central
Government
excluding education,
health, police, and
off-budget agencies
28,585

Population (000)	2,100
Labor force as % of pop.	46.6%
Education emp. as % of pop.	1.6%
Health emp. as % of pop.	1.1%

Source: World Bank staff files.

Defense staff members are reported to have received special payments, with some enhancement from revenues received from donor organizations. Further flexibility is provided, because some positions are classified as "specific posts," allowing wages to be set at a higher rate (for example, administrative inspectors at the Ministry of Justice, labor inspectors, and some police).

It is probable that pay at lower levels is comparable to that in the private sector, particularly after the relative job security afforded by public administration is taken into account, while pay at senior levels is less competitive. Ironically, a weak private sector labor market has, for the time being, eased the difficulty of attracting and retaining qualified people in the public sector. According to the data in Figure A2.4 and Table A2.7, average central government wages relative to GDP per capita were relatively high at approximately 1.8 times GDP per capita in 1999.

Personnel management is weak. In addition to the structural pay problems, attracting, retaining, and motivating qualified staff is difficult because of limited career growth prospects. There are very few promotions, and limited resources and attention devoted to systematically upgrading the skills of staff through either formal or informal (such as on-the-job) training. Most staff are hired to position rather than being promoted. While there are important advantages in permitting and encouraging competition for open positions, the effective absence of reasonable prospects for career advancement reflecting higher salaries undermines the public sector's capacity to attract and retain qualified and highly motivated staff. It does not appear that central authorities exercise much oversight of the personnel management authority exercised by line ministries, nor do there appear to be particularly effective mechanisms for staff to challenge personnel management actions.

There are severe political difficulties in reform. The government has neither the data nor the political will to manage any political backlash that would result from making reductions in force aimed at reducing the wage bill. Under these circumstances, it is not surprising to see the government responding to external pressures for it to reduce the wage bill by seriously considering, and sometimes adopting, untargeted or poorly targeted measures for achieving reductions in force.

There is evidence of sector-specific overstaffing in health and education. Together these sectors account for about 58 percent of government employment. In health, employment of both medical personnel and support staff is excessive relative to demand for services. In education, numbers of nonteaching staff in elementary and secondary schools are higher than levels commonly found in Organisation for Economic Co-operation and Development (OECD) countries, and there are indications that teaching staff is underutilized.

3. Recent and Current Institutional Reforms

Both the Bank and the Fund have been working with the Government of the FYR of Macedonia for several years on institutional and structural reforms. The Fund has focused on keeping the wage bill under control in order to ensure macroeconomic stability, with corresponding implications for downsizing. In particular, under the enhanced structural adjustment facility (ESAF), and later under the PRGF-EFF arrangements, the Fund specified wage ceilings and actively sought the divestment of noncore activities under the PRGF-EFF–supported program.

The Bank has focused on longer-term budget management reforms by working to develop both policy and budget-formulation institutional practices and capacities. This involves bringing various off-budget financing within the budget, creating contestability in the budget preparation and policy formulation process, and strengthening basic accounting and auditing rules, procedures, and capacities. Civil service reforms will continue to focus on creating a depoliticized, merit-based civil service, and making the salary structure within the civil service more competitive and more motivating. The future direction of civil service reform is uncertain following the recent Peace Framework Agreement between ethnic Albanians and Macedonians, which calls for increased participation of ethnic Albanians in the civil service.

Table A2.7 FYR Macedonia: The Main Dimensions of the Public Sector Wage Bill (all units are local currency, 1999)

	Nominal LCU[a]	Percent of GDP	Percent of government expenditure
Total Civilian Central Government and Armed Forces Wage Bill (millions)	17,757	9.1	39.0
Memo items:			
GDP (millions)	195,284		
GDP per capita	96,634		
Total central government expenditure (millions)	45,581		

a. LCU is local currency unit.
Source: IMF Staff Report, April 2000; and WB World Development Indicators database.

4. Key Macrofiscal Concerns

The government has been pursuing wage bill reductions under its agreements with the Fund (see Table A2.7). The Bank has offered considerable advice to the government on how to target the employment reductions required to achieve those targets. The government has made commitments to the Fund to meet reduction targets in the wage bill within tight time frames but has then tended to postpone employment reduction decisions. Last-minute efforts to meet targets in the wage bill have sometimes relied on ad hoc decision rules. In the eyes of the Macedonian public and public employees, such ad hoc measures have tended to equate institutional and governance reforms with reductions in public employment.

5. Need for Including Civil Service Reforms in PRSC and PRGF Programs?

Civil service reform is an essential element to the Public Sector Management Adjustment Credit/Loan [for FYR Macedonia] (PSMAC)–supported reforms. The PSMAC is similar to a PRSC. Key objectives of the reform effort are to (a) make the civil service more meritocratic and less politicized, and (b) make it a more attractive career option, while (c) ensuring a fiscally sustainable public sector.

6. Benchmarks for the Future. How Will Progress Be Monitored?

The government will provide baseline measurements on six monitoring indicators as part of satisfying the monitoring indicators condition for presentation of the Public Sector Management Adjustment Credit (PSMAC 1) to the Board of Directors of the International Development Association (IDA). These indicators include employment and wage bill totals, policy management arrangements, realism of budget requests, treasury system, health service delivery, and civil service management.

Mali

1. Size and Structure of Civilian Central Government

**Figure A2.5 The Main Components of Government
Employment in Mali, 1999**

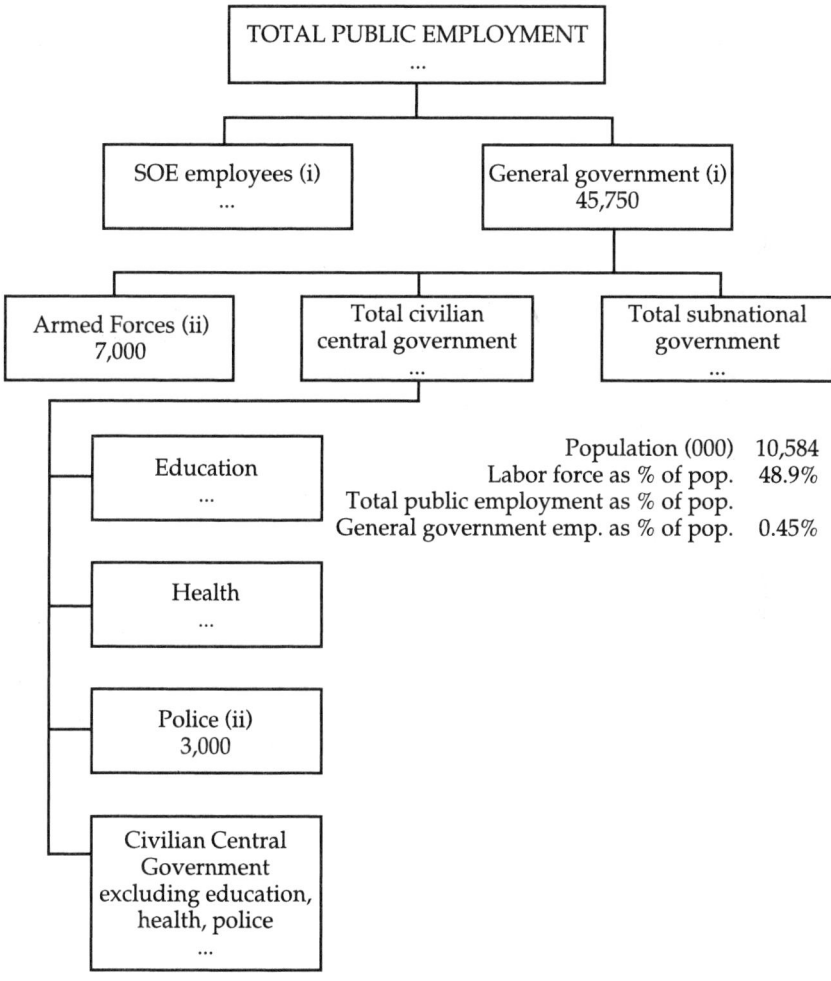

... = not available.

Sources: (i) IMF RED tables (estimate) in 2000 Staff Report; (ii) Updated WB database
on PS employment—1996–99. If no source is shown, then the total is calculated arithmetically.

2. Key Institutional and Structural Concerns

Two major structural problems characterize Malian civil service today: (a) aging of the work force, and (b) poor working conditions, mainly due to budgetary constraints. The combined effects of these problems are low morale and motivation, resulting in poor performance, lack of accountability, and poor public service delivery.

New hiring has been highly restricted in Mali since 1982, with the exception of the health and education sectors. During the last three years, recruitments have been limited to 250 civil servants a year. This policy, while helping to control the wage bill, is producing a dramatic aging of the civil service. The average staff age is 48 years and the mandatory retirement age is 55 years. If maintained, this policy will result in 70 percent of current civil servants being forced to retire within 10 years.

3. Recent and Current Institutional Reforms

The retirement fund (CRM) is facing liquidity problems and was dependent on government transfers of some CFA franc 8 billion in 2000. A CRM reform plan was prepared on the basis of the recommendations of an audit completed in 2000, with technical assistance from the Bank. This plan, which is currently being implemented, will lead to improved transparency in the fund's operations and will facilitate completion of the actuarial study.

Three key public sector reforms—financial sector, privatization, and decentralization—have been initiated in recent years, but with very limited impact so far. Discussion of decentralization has also underscored the trade-offs between "frontal" civil service reform—with all the political risks it entails—and the potential gains from a more pragmatic, incremental approach to reform—working at the heart of intergovernmental relations (administrative, financial, and fiscal relations). Policymakers are well aware of the hard decisions to be made regarding

Table A2.8 Mali: Average Wages, 1998

	Nominal LCU[a]	Ratio of average wage to per capita GDP
Average Government Wage	1,572,000	10.6

a. LCU is local currency unit.
Source: Updated WB database on PS employment—1996–99.

the need to confront an entrenched central bureaucracy unwilling to give up its control over both internal (national budget) and external resources (externally funded investment programs). Another difficulty comes from the need to ensure that a sustainable local government system is put in place, because so far the transfer of mandates and authority to local governments has not been matched with financial resources and fiscal authority.

4. Key Macrofiscal Concerns

The wage bill is not expected to be a source of imbalances in Mali, in light of the need to observe the convergence criterion set out by the West African Economic and Monetary Union (WAEMU)—see Table A2.9. In addition, the ongoing reform of the CRM is expected to address its liquidity problems, and thus eliminate (or limit) the need for government transfers beyond 2002. Yet it is unclear, at this stage, how government transfers to the CRM, if they continue, will tilt the composition of expenditure in the future.

While the restricted hiring of civil servants in recent years, combined with the government's conservative wage policy, improved public finances and resulted in some savings, it only led to a modest shift in public spending toward key social sectors.

Table A2.9 Mali: The Main Dimensions of the Public Sector Wage Bill (all units are local currency, 1999)

	Nominal LCU	Percent of GDP	Percent of government expenditure
Total Civilian Central Government and Armed Forces Wage Bill (millions)	65,300	4.1	15.6
Memo items:			
GDP (millions)	1,604,374		
GDP per capita	147,365		
Total central government expenditure (millions)	419,800		

Sources: IMF RED tables; and WB World Development Indicators database for population.

5. Need for Including Civil Service Reform in PRSC and PRGF Programs?

The second annual program under the PRGF includes a civil service reform component aimed at modernizing the service and harmonizing the various salary structures. However, this reform does not currently benefit from expertise from either the Bank or any other donor. The reform should be an integral part of adjustment lending operations but should be accompanied by other administrative reforms and improvements in transparency and accountability. The main motivation for the reform stems from:

- **Poor public service delivery and deficient resource allocation.** Despite substantial increases in resources allocated to education (2.75 percent of GDP) and to health care (2 percent of GDP) during 1995–98, only modest improvements in services have been achieved: resources are still disproportionately spent in urban areas, while most of the poor live in rural areas. Legislation is passed but is not implemented adequately.

- **Endemic corruption.** A recent study of corruption in the public service in Mali identified three key contributing factors to corruption among civil servants: (a) excessive discretionary power in the hands of civil servants; (b) mild sanctions and lack of safeguards; and (c) lack of transparency of government affairs. Mali lacks a "rule of law" culture (aggravated by a weak judiciary with inadequate human and financial resources to function properly—less than 1 percent of the national budget is allocated to the judiciary). This, and a lack of proper controls on the executive, lead to abuses of power, lack of transparency, and unlimited opportunities for corruption.

6. Benchmarks for the Future. How Will Progress Be Monitored?

Although relevant, reductions in the size of the civil service and compression of the government wage bill are not useful benchmarks to assess progress in institutional reforms. Rather, the focus should be on improvements in service delivery measures, including quantitative targets for the quality and coverage of publicly provided goods and services.

Mongolia

1. Size and Structure of Civilian Central Government

**Figure A2.6 The Main Components of Government
Employment in Mongolia, 2000**

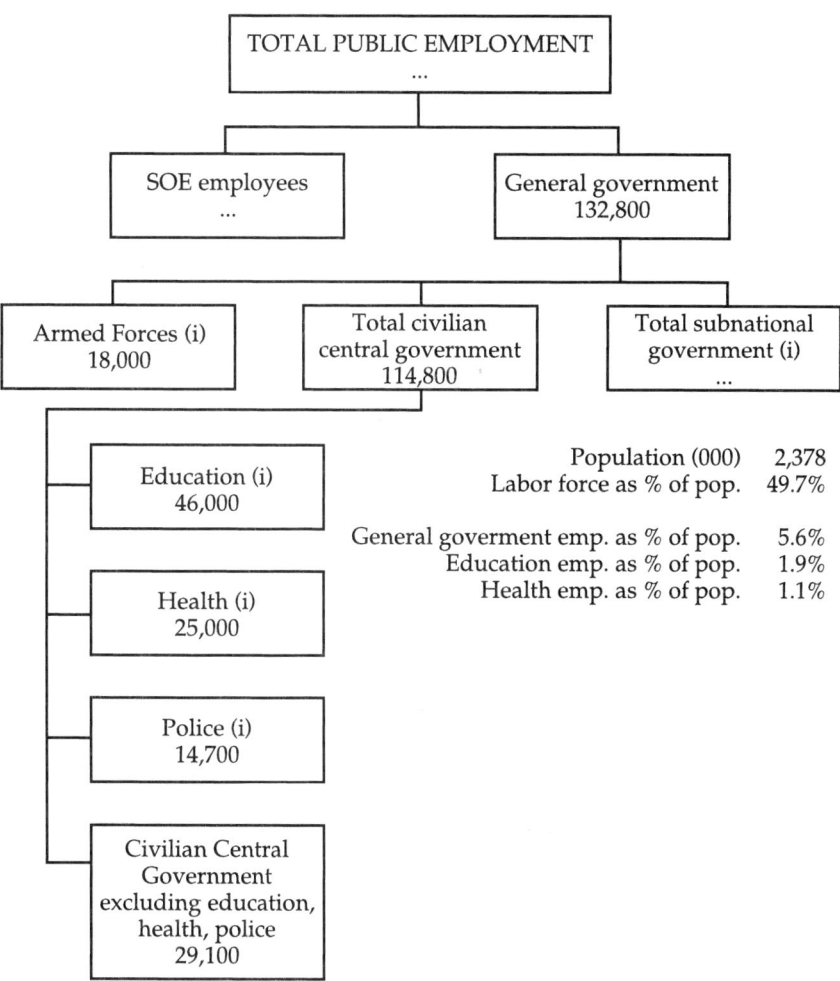

Population (000)   2,378
Labor force as % of pop.   49.7%

General goverment emp. as % of pop.   5.6%
Education emp. as % of pop.   1.9%
Health emp. as % of pop.   1.1%

Sources: (i) World Bank and Mongolia MOF data, courtesy of Vera Songwe. If no source is shown, then the total is calculated arithmetically. (ii) Note that employment in health and education is mostly administered by local governments.

Detailed payroll data on the age composition of the civil service, the grade levels, and number of civil servants in each grade are not readily available. Mongolia has 21 local governments, which administer approximately 60 percent of the wage bill. Although this money is allocated by the central government, local governments have autonomy over their budgets and frequently depart from policies designed by the central government. Budget norms are only indicative and do not restrict local governments in their decisions to hire new staff. Wage policy is determined by the central government, but there is very little control over wage levels in local governments. Indeed, the lack of accountability of local governments over their employment policies is a major factor hampering fiscal consolidation in Mongolia. In education, for example, local governments have the ability to hire staff, with the constraint that budget allocations are made on the basis of agreed on norms determining the student-teacher ratio for each class size and grade, and type of education.

The average monthly salary in the civil service is about US$47 (see Table A2.10). Civil service salaries are on average about 40–50 percent lower than in the private sector.

2. Key Institutional and Structural Concerns

Wage increases have been carried out independently of the overall fiscal aggregates, which have sharply, but disproportionately, raised the costs of public employment. Current institutional arrangements are deficient because they do not institute strict rules for hiring and dismissing civil servants. Over 30 percent of civilian central government is replaced following elections, leading to increased rent seeking. Recruitment into the civil service is no longer based on an entrance examination; thus the overall quality of the staff has declined, particularly in education and in rural areas.

Low requirements for reporting on public employment and wages have de facto limited the monitoring of the civil service.

Table A2.10 Mongolia: Average Wages, 2000

	Nominal LCU[a]	Ratio of average wage to per capita GDP
Average Government Wage	630,658	1.45

a. LCU is local currency unit.
Sources: WB; and Mongolia MoF data.

3. Recent and Current Institutional Reforms

The Public Sector Reform Agenda of the government, under discussion with the IFIs, includes a move toward output-oriented budget management and a change in civil service arrangements toward more merit-based recruitment and promotion.

A newly proposed Privatization Program, vaguely consistent with the public reform agenda, may privatize large segments of the health and education sectors. As an expenditure-saving measure in 2001, the government began the privatization of over 18 institutes of higher learning, and some health-care facilities in the urban areas. This is expected to reduce the overall civil service wage bill. However, the effects of these policies on service delivery need to be examined more closely.

4. Key Macrofiscal Concerns

Current expenditures rose sharply from 18.5 percent of GDP in 1995 to 30 percent of GDP in 2000. The wage bill has also drifted upward, rising to 8.2 percent of GDP in 2000, up from 5 percent in 1995. This is partly due to: (a) successive across-the-board wage increases, which were granted to all civil servants irrespective of productivity; and (b) new hiring of teachers, as required by increasing school enrollment rates, with no compensating retrenchments in lower-priority sectors.

The total wage bill appears excessive in GDP terms and impedes the government from adopting an appropriately differentiated wage structure (see Table A2.11). The relatively low salaries of skilled employees are leading to an overall drop in the quality of the civil service as better-qualified employees move to the private sector. The government has been struggling to retain competent staff by increasing allowances to higher-level staff and allocating training and travel grants.

5. Need for Including Civil Service Reforms in PRSC and PRGF Programs?

The programmatic nature of the PRSC provides an appropriate vehicle for discussing issues of civil service reform. It provides a direct link between the functional analysis of the budget expected of the PRSP and the overall objective of fiscal sustainability. Initial work has been undertaken in the ongoing Public Expenditure Review (PER).

Civil service reforms will be key to the effective implementation of the PRGF program, and an essential part of engineering significant expenditure savings over the medium term, improving fiscal transparency and the effectiveness of public spending. Recent program negotiations

Table A2.11 Mongolia: The Main Dimensions of the Public Sector Wage Bill (all units are local currency, 2000)

	Nominal LCU[a]	Percent of GDP	Percent of government expenditure
Total Civilian Central Government and Armed Forces Wage Bill (millions)	34,748	3.3	9.3
Memo items:			
GDP (millions)	1,044,581		
GDP per capita	439,209		
Total central government expenditure (millions)	373,400		

a. LCU is local currency unit.
Sources: IMF staff; and WB *World Development Indicators* database for population.

include (a) stricter standards for fiscal data reporting, (b) policies to restrain wage increases in 2001 and contain the wage bill over 2002–04, and (c) support for development of a long-term strategy with Bank collaboration.

6. Benchmarks for the Future. How Will Progress Be Monitored?

Benchmarks for the future include (a) revising the civil service code and developing policies for creating a professional civil service with transparent rules for hiring and firing; (b) developing a fully functioning payroll system; (c) ensuring that the forthcoming reforms to the budget process facilitate the coordination of civil service reforms among government agencies; and (d) rationalizing the level of the civil service, with a view to decreasing the overall size the wage bill, while increasing the quality of services delivered.

Pakistan

1. Size and Structure of Civilian Central Government

Civil service employees of civilian central government (see Figure A2.7) receive a basic monthly salary, a variety of allowances (equal to 25–40 percent of base pay), and—for some—benefits in-kind, such as housing and transport. These civil servants also enjoy a pension, which is not common in the private sector.

Once admitted to a particular civil service cadre, staff (district management, secretariat, taxation, customs, technical cadres, and so on) progress on the basis of seniority. Lateral entry is uncommon. An elite core of generalists (district management and secretariat groups) is managed separately.

2. Key Institutional and Structural Concerns

Base pay for the vast majority of government employees is according to a single pay scale. However, there are numerous cash allowances (and in-kind benefits for high-level civil servants). These allowances and benefits can total as much as 400 percent or more of basic salary (see Table A2.12).

In 1998, fewer than 10 percent of federal government employees were paid by means of a computerized payroll. There were at least 48 allowances in existence, greatly complicating the manual payroll system. Incorporating these allowances into base pay would both simplify the payroll system and make it far more transparent.

3. Recent and Current Institutional Reforms

The Government of Pakistan (GoP) believes that substantial devolution of government functions to the local governments (LGOs) is essential for improving accountability and service delivery in the country. The government has proposed a new system with three layers of local bodies at the district, *tehsil*, and union levels. These plans for devolution were scheduled to become effective on August 14, 2001. Devolution is to be implemented in phases over the next three years. There are important signs of commitment of the president to combat the patronage and pervasive political interference in appointments and transfers, as well as the opaque, overly generous pension system.

The low quality of public services in Pakistan reflects, in the authorities' view, the low capacity of the civil service, because of skills shortage,

Figure A2.7 The Main Components of Government Employment in Pakistan, 2000

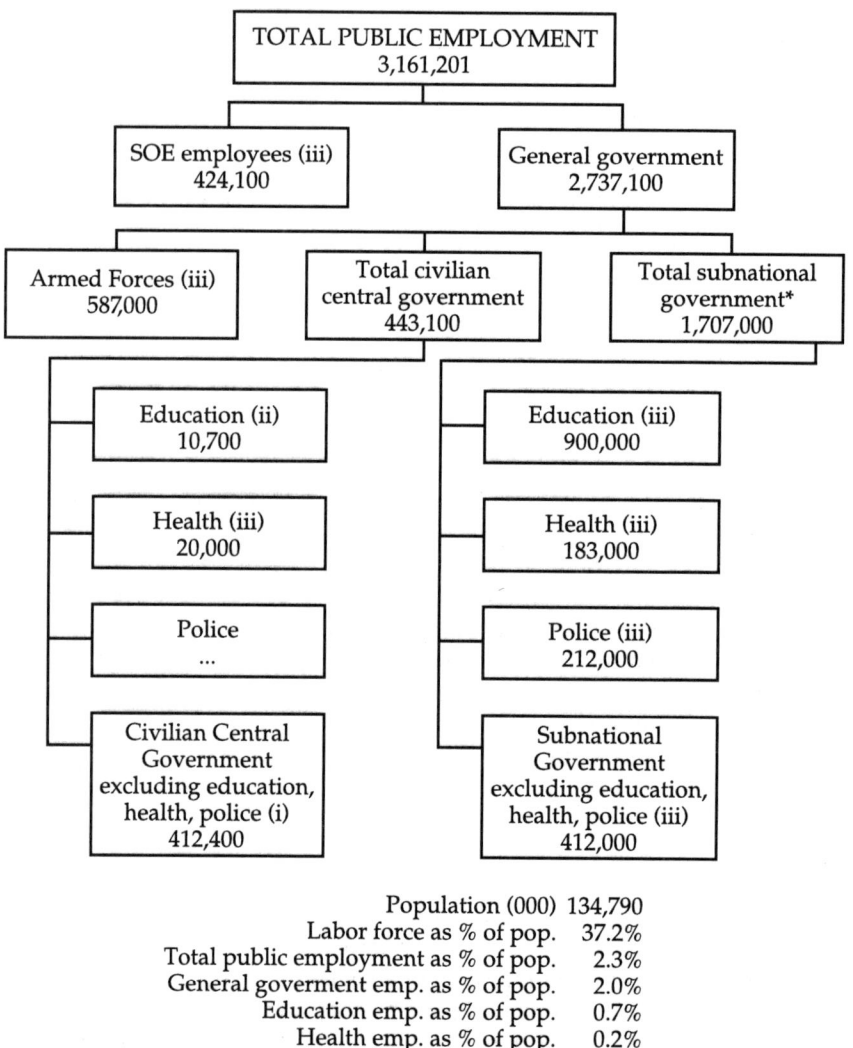

Population (000) 134,790
Labor force as % of pop.   37.2%
Total public employment as % of pop.   2.3%
General goverment emp. as % of pop.   2.0%
Education emp. as % of pop.   0.7%
Health emp. as % of pop.   0.2%

Sources and dates covered: (i) Government of Pakistan, Establishment Division. This may be a slight understatement as it excludes civilian staffs in the Ministry of Defence, the Ministry of Foreign Affairs, and certain Public Sector Organizations/Corporations; (ii) Government of Pakistan, Planning Commission report, April 2000; (iii) Updated WB database on PS employment—1996–99; data are for 1997, assumed relatively unchanged for 2000. If no source is shown, then the total is calculated arithmetically. *Provincial employment figures are based on numbers of sanctioned posts rather than actual employment.

Table A2.12 Pakistan: Average Wages, 1998

	Nominal LCU[a]	Ratio of average wage to per capita GDP
Average Government Wage[1]	43,634	1.85

1. This average is derived from federal provincial personnel expenditures.
a. LCU is local currency unit.

Note: Pakistan's public administration has a highly centralized organizational structure, management, and rules. Patronage undermines the Weberian rules that formally underlie Pakistan's civil service. Performance evaluations are not meaningful for promotions and rewards. Staff automatically "move over" to the next higher grade within two years after they have reached the maximum of the pay scale for their existing grade. In general, relatively low pay appears to be no barrier to recruiting well-qualified people at entry level.

Source: "A Framework for Civil Service Reform in Pakistan." World Bank Report No. 18386-PAK, December 15, 1998.

lack of incentive structure for better performance, quota-based employment, politicization, and vested interests. To address these problems, the government has launched a civil service reform that relies on educational programs; the review of salary structure; the introduction of a promotion system that is based on merit; and across-the-board downsizing through early retirement measures.

4. Key Macrofiscal Concerns

The size of the wage bill, while not figuring prominently in the macroeconomic dialogue, has been a major source of concern in the policy dialogue on provincial economic reforms (see Table A2.13). Wage bills and pensions can account for more than 40 percent of provincial government expenditures. However, in the context of the ongoing federal pay and pension reform, more attention must be given to the wage bill dynamics, given that a very important pay increase is involved (first estimate of the cost for the full-year impact of the reform is about 1 percent of GDP). This goes together with a pension reform and a downsizing of the civil service for which the costs and the advantages have not yet been clearly estimated.

The composition of spending is mainly affected by interest payments on debt (about 50 percent of federal current expenditure, and 7 percent in GDP terms) and defense spending (close to 33 percent of federal current expenditure, and 4.5 in GDP terms). Development spending at both federal and provincial levels has been constrained to below 3 percent of

GDP. The bulk of government employment is concentrated at the provincial level.

At both the fiscal and the balance of payments (BOP) levels, most of the imbalances are linked to the difficult debt situation faced by Pakistan. During the last year, in the context of the SBA, the country has benefited from debt rescheduling and has undertaken some fiscal consolidation, though unfavorable weather conditions will limit the amount of fiscal adjustment affordable by the country in fiscal 2001–02.

5. Need for Including Civil Service Reforms in the PRSC and PRGF Programs?

The PRSP process is scheduled to begin this year in Pakistan. Civil service reforms at the federal and provincial government levels will likely appear prominently in this process, because both are central to the government's devolution initiative, intended to enhance efficiency, accountability, and the quality of service delivery to local communities. Civil service reform issues will be a core part of the provincial reform programs in provinces such as Sindh and North Western Frontier Province (NWFP) that are likely to be supported by adjustment lending.

A mission was in Pakistan in the second half of August 2001 to conclude the third (and last) review of the SBA and start negotiation for a medium-term program that could be supported by the PRGF. Civil ser-

Table A2.13 Pakistan: The Main Dimensions of the Public Sector Wage Bill (all units are local currency, 1999)

	Nominal LCU[a]	Percent of GDP	Percent of government expenditure
Total Civilian Central Government Wage Bill (millions)[1]	23,910	0.75	3.3
Memo items:			
GDP (millions)[2]	3,182,000		
GDP per capita[3]	23,607		
Total central government expenditure (millions)	728,700		

a. LCU is local currency unit.

Sources: 1. IMF staff; 2. IMF Staff Report, March 2001, EBS/01/39; 3. WB World Development Indicators database.

vice reform will be included in the PRGF-supported program, but will not be part of its conditionality, given that the Bank will take the lead on advising the government and monitoring the structural aspect of the reform. The Fund will limit its role to monitoring the fiscal implications of the reform. One issue that will need particular attention is the possibility of higher-than-estimated fiscal costs over the medium term of the devolution program.

6. Benchmarks for the Future.
How Will Progress Be Monitored?

To address risks in devolving authority for delivery of resources and financial management from the provincial to local governments, expenditure will be tracked under the proposed Structural Adjustment Credit for Pakistan (WB Report No. P7443-PAK). Financial transfers will be based on: (a) need (based on population); (b) "backwardness" (based on housing units and statistics); and (c) performance (fiscal and service delivery—such as girls' primary school enrollment).

The Russian Federation

1. Size and Structure of Civilian Central Government

The nearest approximation to civil servant status in Russia is afforded to the "state service" positions in the federal executive branch, covered under federal law no. 119-FZ of July 31, 1995. At a total of some 519,000, the state service is a relatively modest proportion of total public employment in Russia. Excluding employment in state-owned enterprises, for which there are no current data, total public employment in Russia is approximately 6.4 million (see Figure A2.8).

A small number of state service officials are located in Moscow-based ministries and other federal executive bodies. The remainder, although employed by the federal government, are located in "subjects of the Russian Federation," rayons, and municipalities. Excluding the assumed 150,000 employees of the Ministries of Defense and Interior, the state service officials in Moscow represent only some 7 percent of the total civilian central government.

2. Key Institutional and Structural Concerns

Rewards structure does not motivate. Total rewards for officials in the state service include monetary payments and in-kind benefits, although these are increasingly restricted to a very small number of senior officials. Salaries and allowances are governed by two scales for headquarters offices (for ministries and for other executive bodies) and four scales for local office staff, classified according to the size of the Federation subject, rayon, or municipality in which they are located. The resulting pattern of rewards is highly complex and unlikely to motivate.

Total compensation is inadequate. There are few sound comparators for senior state servant salaries, but it seems probable that official monetary rewards are significantly below those that might be obtained in the private sector. Russian experts estimate that at the level of deputy ministers, official monetary rewards are between 10 to 15 times below those in the private sector in Moscow. In 1998, average wages in the central government were rubles (Rub) 47,583, about 2.54 times the per capita GDP. There are few data available on rewards for public officials outside of the state service.

Merit is not rewarded. The state service will perhaps form the foundation of a formal merit-based civil service, but currently this group includes the judiciary, excludes administrators in the Ministries of Defense and Interior, and has no merit-protection body to ensure competence and political neutrality.

Figure A2.8 The Main Components of Government Employment in Russia, 1998

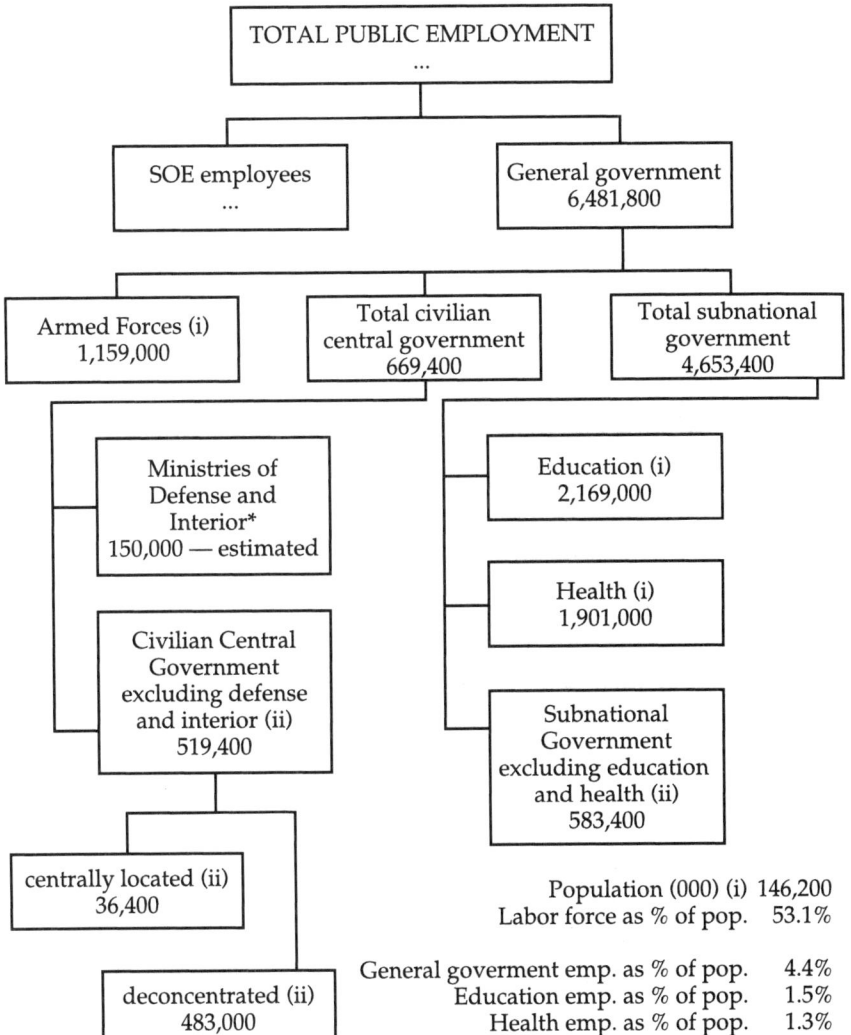

TOTAL PUBLIC EMPLOYMENT
...

SOE employees
...

General government
6,481,800

Armed Forces (i)
1,159,000

Total civilian
central government
669,400

Total subnational
government
4,653,400

Ministries of
Defense and
Interior*
150,000 — estimated

Education (i)
2,169,000

Health (i)
1,901,000

Civilian Central
Government
excluding defense
and interior (ii)
519,400

Subnational
Government
excluding education
and health (ii)
583,400

centrally located (ii)
36,400

Population (000) (i) 146,200
Labor force as % of pop.   53.1%

General goverment emp. as % of pop.   4.4%
deconcentrated (ii)
483,000
Education emp. as % of pop.   1.5%
Health emp. as % of pop.   1.3%

Sources: (i) Updated WB database on PS employment—dates between 1996–99; (ii) Goskomstat (1998). *Estimated figure. If no source shown, then the total is calculated arithmetically.

3. Recent and Current Institutional Reforms

Civil service reform to date has focused on the judiciary and the military. Current wage bills for these groups are estimated at Rub 5.5 billion (0.2 percent of GDP) and Rub 9.3 billion (0.4 percent of GDP), respectively. An estimated 400,000 reduction in military personnel is programmed for 2002. Some reform measures were implemented in 1998 with some reductions in 1999. In 1998 cuts of 275,000 personnel were made across the public sector, of which 155,000 were cut from the military. There was no direct involvement of the IFIs in preparing the reforms.

A concept for modernization of the Federal Civil Service is likely to be approved soon and could lead to a detailed action plan. President Putin has recently signed an executive order creating a commission to reform the State Service, headed by the prime minister. He has also created an interministerial working group to prepare drafts of the program for civil service reform, for adjusting federal laws, as well as other normative acts related to civil service. The working group will be headed by the first deputy head of the president's administration. Much of the current discussion focuses on possible efficiency improvements in pay and employment reforms in the state service. On savings, it is clear that there are relatively few opportunities for efficiency improvements in the Moscow offices of the federal ministries and other executive bodies. A reduction in the numbers of state servants seems unwise and somewhat unproductive, given their relatively small number.

Pay increases for the state service would have a relatively modest impact on the Federal Government wage bill. However, it is not clear what the impact of such increases would be on other groups of staff and any race toward maintaining parity could prove fiscally unsustainable. In particular, the proposed unified tariff schedule (UTS) wage system aims to unify base pay and additional payment benefits, by awarding pay increases and eliminating allowances. This proposed pay increase poses no immediate or medium-term problems to the federal government budget, but it does pose a problem at the subnational level, where savings from subnational reforms will take longer to materialize. As a result, the overall picture suggests that public sector wages may grow too rapidly following the planned wage increase.

The government is considering functional reviews as one avenue for pursuing this further. The institutional reform agenda is likely to include the establishment of a formal, merit-based civil service, and, as noted, this would include a tighter legal definition of the civil service, and the establishment of a merit-protection body to ensure competence and political neutrality.

4. Key Macrofiscal Concerns

In 1998, the authorities adopted a program for controlling government spending in the face of external and domestic imbalances, including a large budget deficit (6 percent of GDP). They followed prudent policies in 1999–2001 with a surplus of 2.5 percent of GDP projected for 2001. The draft 2002 budget envisages a surplus of 1.5 percent of GDP. However, revenues have been supported by high global energy prices, and the staff is concerned about the medium-term outlook owing to the cost of reforms (tax policy, pensions, judiciary, wage, education, health, and social benefits).

The wage bill appears sustainable at the federal level but may be more problematic at the subnational level (see Table A2.14). In 1997 and 1998 the federal wage bill was equivalent to 3.2 percent of GDP. Following cuts in real wages in response to the crisis as well as cuts in employment in 1998 and 1999, the federal government wage bill was reduced to Rub 118

Table A2.14 Russia: The Main Dimensions of the Public Sector Wage Bill (all units are local currency, 1999)

	Nominal LCU[a]	Percent of GDP	Percent of government expenditure
Total Civilian Central Government Wage Bill (millions)	69,970	1.5	8.6
Armed Forces Wage Bill (millions)	48,200	1.1	5.9
Total Civilian Central Government and Armed Forces Wage Bill (millions)	118,170	2.6	14.5
Memo items:			
GDP (millions)	4,545,489		
GDP per capita	30,762		
Total central government expenditure (millions)	812,900		

a. LCU is local currency unit.

Sources: Government Financial Statistics (GFS) 1999; IMF RED tables; and WB *World Development Indicators* database for population.

billion in 1999, about 2.6 percent of GDP and about 14.5 percent of federal government expenditure. In 2002 large wage increases related to pay reform and reform of the military and judiciary will increase the wage bill to 2.9 percent of GDP. The pay increase is linked to a shift in spending toward the social sectors from 2.2 percent to 2.5 percent of GDP and from 18 percent to 21 percent of noninterest expenditure.

5. Need for Including Civil Service Reforms in PRSC and PRGF Programs?

Russia is not a PRGF country and no other program is currently in place. As a middle-income country, Russia is not required to prepare a PRSP. However, the authorities are continuing with civil service reform, and are extremely keen to receive technical support and policy advice on this from the IFIs.

6. Benchmarks for the Future. How Will Progress Be Monitored?

The Bank does not anticipate any major lending operation to the Russian Federation concerning civil service reform although there is a possibility of a lending operation to support subnational public administration reform in fiscal 2003 or fiscal 2004. Monitoring will be undertaken within the intensive technical assistance that the Bank is providing. Progress will be monitored by the Fund in the context of regular surveillance, including currently under post program monitoring.

Tanzania

1. Size and Structure of Civilian Central Government

Total public employment in 1999 was approximately 450,000 (see Figure
A2.9). Recent decentralization has resulted in the devolution of centrally
managed education and health personnel, but has not removed them

**Figure A2.9 The Main Components of Government
Employment in Tanzania, 1999**

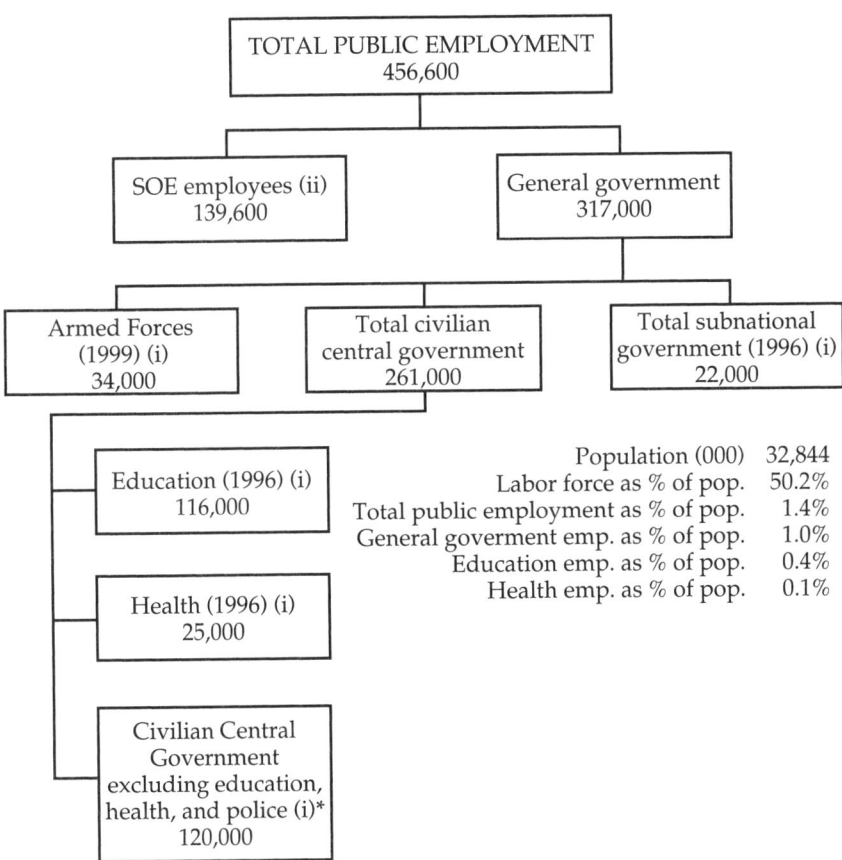

Sources: (i) Updated WB database on PS employment—1996–99; *1996 data adjusted to
1999 on the basis of WB file data; (ii) 1999 Government of Tanzania Economic Survey. If no
source is shown, then the total is calculated arithmetically.

from the central government wage bill. Some ministry staffs, for example, agriculture, have been fully decentralized and are now funded from local government budgets.

2. Key Institutional and Structural Concerns

Capacity and performance have been undermined by low pay and associated informality, with a weak work ethos. Although civil service employment almost tripled between 1971–72 and 1993–94, the wage bill was kept under control by sharp erosion in real wages. The effect of this decline on the quality of public services was further aggravated by a deliberate compression of the wage scale, with even sharper reductions in real wages for technical and professional staff. The wage bill remains a significant fiscal burden and the take-home pay has not sufficiently improved for technical and professional staff. The salaries of top-level civil servants are generally supplemented by donors, but the remuneration of technical and professional staff remains a factor of 10 below wages in nonbudgetary government institutions, such as the Central Bank. As a result, the government has great difficulties in attracting and retaining qualified professional staff, and the effectiveness of much technical assistance in the macrofiscal area is impaired because of the lack of qualified national counterparts. The average government wage across central government is Tanzanian shillings (T Sh) 861.5 thousand; this is 4.3 times larger than per capita GDP.

In the education and health sectors, a reallocation of current staff could achieve better distribution in rural areas. Still, absolute numbers are insufficient in relation to service delivery targets.

3. Recent and Current Institutional Reforms

The strength of the main political party, the Chama Cha Mapinduzi (Revolutionary Party) of Tanzania (CCM), with a long history of open debate and discussion, provides considerable discipline in a demanding reform process. The multi-party framework creates a competitive environment, forcing politicians to be serious about the reforms.

The recent track record on civil service reforms has been encouraging. The total number of employees in civilian central government fell from 355,000 to around 260,000 over the last eight years. The pay structure has been rationalized and some decompression achieved, although recent evidence points to the damaging combination of the tax system and the monetization of benefits, which has resulted in a real decrease in wages for many staff. Rationalization of staff through reviews has been extended to local government. Noncore services have been contracted out.

There are two innovative features of the current institutional reforms: (a) agency level restructuring and performance focus, and (b) a pragmatic approach to salary enhancement. Both are showing some promise. Using the incentives provided by a Performance Improvement Fund, eight ministries, departments, and agencies (MDAs) have strategic plans and are working on annual operational plans. The cornerstone of the pay strategy is selected accelerated salary enhancement (SASE). The SASE responds to the challenge of achieving a higher level of reward for public sector employees under severe budgetary constraints, when there is little scope for across-the-board salary enhancement, and when it is clear that employment reduction will not be enough to finance pay strategy targets. This is consistent with the medium-term pay strategy and provides significant pay enhancement for technical or professional staff and for those in critical positions. SASE should facilitate to phase out project implementation units (PIUs) by bringing donor top-ups and project staff salaries in line with medium-term pay reform targets and eventually eliminating them. Thus far, however, SASE is being applied on a pilot basis in only two ministries.

4. Key Macrofiscal Concerns

Tanzania has made excellent progress in stabilizing its economy since 1995. Large fiscal imbalances in 1993–95 were caused by rapid increases in expenditures and stagnating revenues (reflecting increasing exemptions). However, fiscal consolidation under a strict cash-rationing system, supported by tight monetary policies, resulted in a reduction in inflation from almost 30 percent in 1993 to about 5 percent at present, and gross official reserves increased from equivalent to 1.5 months of imports of goods and nonfactor services in 1995 to more than 5 months. Real GDP growth also increased during this period, from 3.6 percent in 1995 to more than 5 percent in 2000. Presently, the key macrofiscal concerns in Tanzania are the continuing low revenue-to-GDP ratio (see Table A2.15), weak expenditure management at the central as well as the local governments levels, and low capacity in macrofiscal analysis and policy formulation.

Tanzania has received assistance in macrofiscal reforms from both the Bank and the Fund. The Bank has played an important role in civil service reform and restructuring and privatizing the parastatal enterprises. In addition, it has been a driving force behind annual PERs and the formulation, with broad participation of donors and civil society, of medium-term expenditure frameworks. The Fund has assisted the authorities in formulating the broad outlines of the annual budgets consistent with the macroeconomic objectives, and in macrofiscal analysis. In addition,

Table A2.15 Tanzania: The Main Dimensions of the Public Sector Wage Bill (all units are local currency, 1998–99)

	Nominal LCU[a]	Percent of GDP	Percent of government expenditure
General Government Wage Bill (millions)	220,480	3.6	24.4
Memo items:			
GDP (millions)	6,114,000		
GDP per capita	187,659		
Total central government expenditure (millions)	905,200		

a. LCU is local currency unit.

Sources: GFS 1999; IMF RED tables; and WB *World Development Indicators* database for population.

FAD has provided extensive technical assistance with regard to public expenditure management. With regard to the latter, FAD is the executing agency for a project financed by Switzerland to strengthen the Policy Analysis Department in the MoF.

5. Need for Including Civil Service Reforms in PRSC and PRGF Programs?

The reform process in Tanzania started before the PRSP exercise, but the I-PRSP reflects the dual concerns for improving wages and strengthening performance management at agency level.

The PRGF in Tanzania has been formulated with a view to allowing sufficient room for wage increases in the context of the medium-term pay reform policy. With increased emphasis on poverty reduction and on transparency and corruption issues, the quality of public services is becoming increasingly important under PRGF-supported programs. Many of these issues are in the domain of the Bank and should be addressed under Bank-supported operations. However, where this is not the case, appropriate conditionality should be included under Fund-supported programs.

6. Benchmarks for the Future.
How Will Progress Be Monitored?

Key Bank indicators include further downsizing of the public sector, and evidence of service delivery improvement as measured by public surveys. More specific indicators include the numbers of performance benchmarks established for MDAs and the number of executive agencies established.

Employment is no longer a major concern for the Fund in Tanzania; indicators and benchmarks are discussed with the authorities during program and surveillance missions. Developments in the wage bill are monitored by Fund staff on a monthly basis in the context of monitoring overall fiscal developments.

The Republic of Yemen

1. Size and Structure of Civilian Central Government

The unification of the Arab Republic of Yemen and the People's Democratic Republic of Yemen in 1990 required the merger of two very different systems, and created a much larger civil service that at times duplicated functions (see Figure A2.10). In addition, the return of around 800,000 Yemenis from the Gulf, following the Gulf War, required the government to absorb a large number into the civil service for social reasons, further exacerbating the problem of overstaffing.

2. Key Institutional and Structural Concerns

There are 13 job grades in the Yemeni civil service. Though the classification system itself is fairly clear, the required educational qualifications are very minimal. Moreover, the legislative framework does not require merit-based recruitment. Even public announcement of vacancies, by law, is only required for positions if the Ministry of Civil Service and Administrative Reform (the Republic of Yemen) (MOCSAR) decides it is essential or if the concerned administrative unit recommends it.

Persons can be promoted from one job grade to the next simply through years of experience, even if their specific job does not change. The general level of educational attainment within the civil service is low. Within the civilian civil service, 13 percent of the permanent staff members are illiterate. Only 1 percent of the civilian civil service holds a graduate degree, an additional 16 percent a bachelors degree, and 23 percent a secondary school degree.

The economic turmoil throughout 1990–95 caused civil service wages to decline substantially in real terms. The overall result is a large, poorly trained and poorly paid public administration. Many ministers estimate that large numbers of their staff are redundant (a commonly cited figure is 50 percent). The recent civil service census, in fact, found that about 35,000 employees say that they are without specific jobs (this also includes political party workers and about 11,000 workers who have been transferred into the civil administration from public enterprises that have been closed).

Average allowances range from approximately one-quarter to one-half of gross pay, depending on the salary grade. Even after factoring in allowances, the ratio of the midpoint of the highest civil service pay scale to the midpoint of the lowest civil service pay scale is only 3.0. Survey results indicate that top managers in the private sector receive nine times

Figure A2.10 The Main Components of Government Employment in the Republic of Yemen, 1999

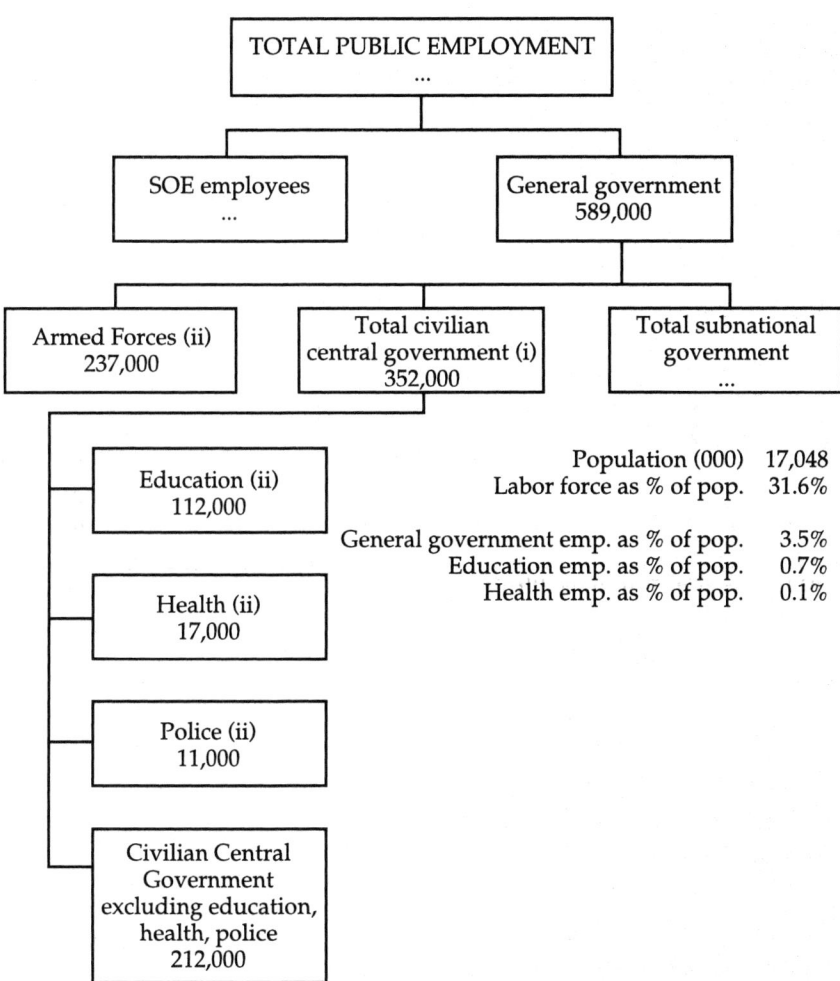

Sources and dates covered: (i) MOCSAR and World Bank calculations. Includes civil administration and contract workers. Approximately 3.6 percent of employees are contract workers. (ii) Updated WB database on PS employment; data are for 1998. If no source is shown, then the total is calculated arithmetically.

Table A2.16 Republic of Yemen: Average Wages, 1999

	Nominal LCU[a]	Ratio of average wage to per capita GDP
Average Government Wage	207,306	4.1

a. LCU is local currency unit.
Source: Calculated from Figure A2.10 and Table A2.17.

the compensation of their public sector counterparts. This imbalance between private sector and public sector wages is reduced for less senior positions, but even at the support services level, private sector compensation was 2.8 times the public sector level (see Table A2.16).

3. Recent and Current Institutional Reforms

Implementation of a wide-ranging structural reform agenda has often been delayed, largely because of the difficulty of mobilizing political support for tough reforms, such as tax and pension reform, particularly in a context of rising oil revenues.

To deal with the labor redundancy problem, legislation was recently passed to establish a civil service fund (CSF) into which redundant employees would be transferred, along with their salaries. In the short term, there would be no cost savings, since staff continue to receive their salaries, but at least they are removed from the employment roster of the line ministry. The aim is to offer CSF staff buy-out packages so that they are permanently removed from the government payroll. This should facilitate restructuring and developing positions and job descriptions for the remaining staff. However, the specific operating rules and procedures needed to make the CSF operational have not yet been established.

The government is presently committed to undertaking civil service reform in selected pilot ministries and agencies, starting in 2001, with a view toward reducing the payroll. It is also preparing to issue biometric cards to all civil servants as a way to identify, and eliminate from the payroll, double-dippers and ghost workers.

4. Key Macrofiscal Concerns

Following unification, the wage bill became a key macrofiscal concern by the mid-1990s, reaching nearly 11 percent of GDP in 1993. Subsequent high inflation eroded the wage bill to 6 percent of GDP by 1997. (By 1996, the average real wage in the public sector was only 15 percent of the 1990 real wage level.) Since then, the government has struggled to contain the wage bill. From 1996 to 1998 a hiring freeze was in place for all sectors except education and health, but the ability to maintain this restraint had evaporated by 1999. A large backlog of unemployed secondary school and college graduates increasingly began to demand jobs in the major urban areas. The government saw increasing public employment as a safety valve to let off the escalating tensions and dissatisfaction among the unemployed, somewhat educated youth. The wage bill rose to 11.5 percent of GDP in 1999 (see Table A2.17).

The government has limited wage increases over the past few years. However, it has also introduced a number of special laws for specific cadres of workers (such as teachers, healthcare workers, and university professors). The purpose of these laws is to introduce special (higher) compensation to these cadres of workers; in some cases the rationale is justified (such as when allowances are introduced to attract teachers to remote areas). The question is whether this trend of bilateral negotiations with individual cadres of civil servants (most recently port workers) will undermine a revision of the civil service pay scale in a fiscally sustainable manner.

Table A2.17 Republic of Yemen: The Main Dimensions of the Public Sector Wage Bill (all units are local currency, 1999)

	Nominal LCU[a]	Percent of GDP	Percent of government expenditure
Total Civilian Central Government Wage Bill (millions)	81,070	7.6	26.1
Armed Forces Wage Bill (millions)	41,033	3.9	13.2
Total Civilian Central Government and Armed Forces Wage Bill (millions)	122,103	11.5	39.3
Memo items:			
GDP (millions)	1,063,557		
GDP per capita	51,035		
Total central government expenditure (millions)	310,702		

a. LCU is local currency unit.
Sources: GFS 1999, IMF RED tables; and WB *World Development Indicators* database for population.

The Fund has provided considerable technical assistance on tax policy and on pension reform. Progress in the tax area has been slow, but the authorities have made progress on a draft pension law that would put the pension system on a sustainable footing. The authorities are awaiting the actuarial results of a follow-up technical assistance (TA) mission to finalize the draft.

5. Need for Including Civil Service Reform in PRSC and PRGF Programs?

The current Fund program included conditionality on civil service reform during 2000, specifically on the retirement of over-age civil servants identified at the end of 1999 by the ongoing Bank project. Explicit conditionality in the area of civil service reform is likely to be shifted to the Bank, but the Fund would continue to seek restraint in the civil service wage bill as part of any program in the years ahead, and would seek to limit real wage increases until progress is made in civil service reform.

6. Benchmarks for the Future. How Will Progress Be Monitored?

Wage bill issues would be monitored as are any other item of government expenditure. This would be the main form of monitoring, in the absence of Fund conditionality in this area.

Zambia

1. Size and Structure of Civilian Central Government

The size of civilian central and subnational government has been reduced from 139,000 in 1998 to about 104,000 today (see Figure A2.11). These reductions exceeded the original target by about 10,000, partly because of the devastating impact of acquired immune deficiency syndrome (AIDS). A study to establish the levels and direction of the required size of the public service was undertaken in 2000 and included proposals, which were subsequently approved by the cabinet, to reduce the size of the civil service to 95,000 and improve salaries for classes of workers that have proved difficult to attract and retain.

2. Key Institutional and Structural Concerns

Effective establishment control mechanisms were put in place three years ago. Each appointment must now go to the head of the civil service for approval. There are few ghosts, because the payroll and establishment lists are now nearly the same. Nevertheless, despite these control mechanisms and previous retrenchment, the wage bill is increasing to levels that are thought to be unsustainable, largely due to strong pressures to increase wages.

The employment and pension rights of public service workers are protected by the constitution. To change their terms of employment would require a change in the constitution or a delinkage of their terms of employment. Public employees are unionized and pressing the government for wage increases in advance of general elections that must take place by December 7, 2001. The ruling party is dependent upon urban votes for its political success, which is where the unions are strong.

It is difficult to hire professional staff given low salaries, though allowances partly make up for this. Average annual salaries range from about US$3,500 for senior managers, US$2,500 for judicial officers, US$2,200 for medical doctors, down to US$600 for nurses (see Table A2.18). Some staff members receive housing allowances, and some senior officers also receive cars and other benefits. There are considerable incentives for petty corruption.

In the education sector, there is a clear shortage of qualified teachers in rural areas. Temporary teachers (approximately 4,500) have been hired to serve in rural areas. Since January 2001 newly trained primary school teachers have not been posted to schools because the Ministry of Education has no money to put them on the payroll.

Figure A2.11 The Main Components of Government Employment in Zambia, 2000

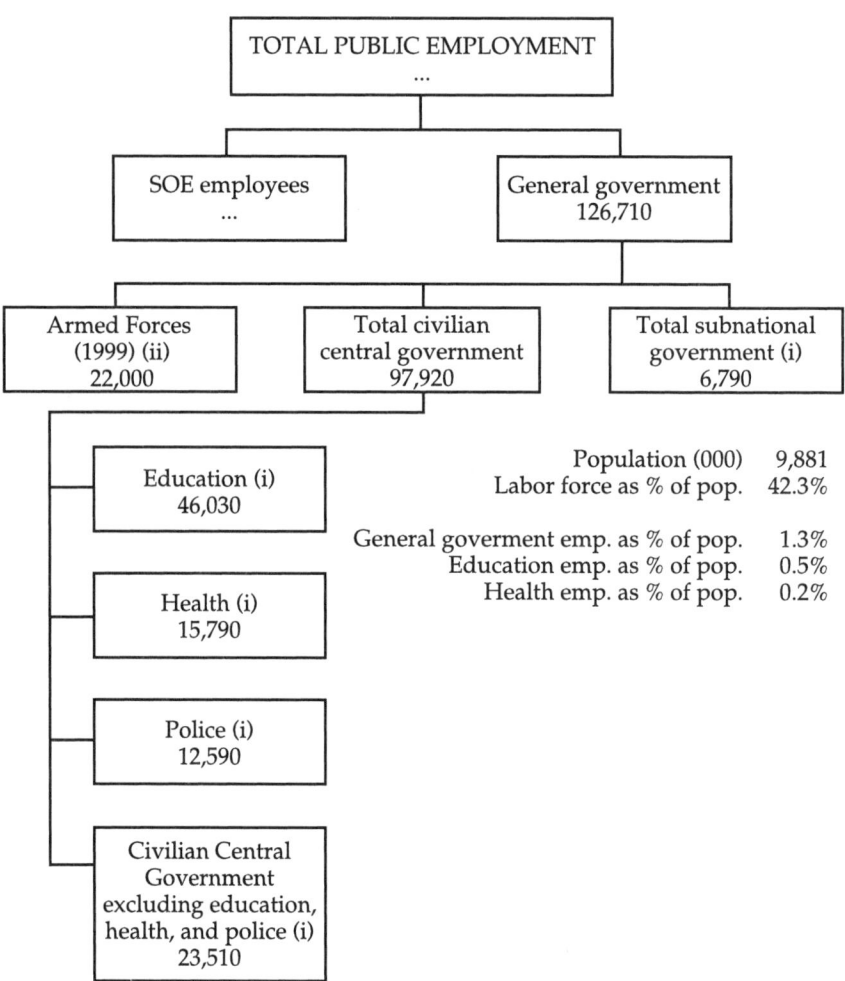

Sources: "Study to Establish the Levels and Direction of the Required Size of the Public Service," March 2000; (ii) Updated WB database on PS employment—1996–99. If no source is shown, then the total is calculated arithmetically.

Table A2.18 Zambia: Average Wages, 1999

	Nominal LCU[a]	Ratio of average wage to per capita GDP
Average Government Wage	3,353,636	4.4

a. LCU is local currency unit.
Source: Calculated from Figure A2.11 and Table A2.19.

3. Recent and Current Institutional Reforms

In the last two years the government of Zambia has "hived off" four public agencies (such as the Wildlife Authority and the National Institute of Public Administration), giving them an independent legislative existence, with the ability to raise revenues, and so on. By agreement, the subventions that these agencies receive from government will be reduced according to specific timetables until they reach zero. This reform reflected a shift in focus for the Bank and the Fund from the number of people to controls on the budget.

The Bank-supported Public Sector Capacity Building Project (PSCAP) sets out to: (a) reduce the government work force and implement a pay reform; (b) prepare the core civil service in policy and public service management; (c) improve financial management, accountability, and transparency; (d) promote judicial and legal reform; and (e) support decentralization. The United Kingdom's Department for International Development has backed the implementation of an electronic payroll system, at a cost of US$9 million.

The Bank's Basic Education Subsector Investment Program Support Project (BESSIP), in conjunction with other bilateral and multilateral agencies, supports teacher training, particularly for rural areas. It will also finance construction of more primary schools, which should lead to hiring more teachers.

4. Key Macrofiscal Concerns

Zambia's total central government wage bill reached 5.4 percent of GDP in 2000, but is poised to be significantly higher in 2001, for the reasons cited above (see Table A2.19). The wage bill is still relatively modest compared with those of other anglophone African countries. However, it is the single largest expenditure item in Zambia's domestic budget. (Education makes up 50 percent of the wage bill, health 18 percent, and the police 11 percent.) Reducing the wage bill in order to allow increased spending on

Table A2.19 Zambia: The Main Dimensions of the Public Sector Wage Bill (all units are local currency, 1999)

	Nominal LCU[a]	Percent of GDP	Percent of government expenditure
Total Civilian Central Government Wage Bill (millions)[1]	311,002	4.1	14.2
Armed Forces Wage Bill (millions)	91,166	1.2	4.2
Total Civilian Central Government and Armed Forces Wage Bill (millions)	402,168	5.4	18.3
Memo items:			
GDP (millions)	7,515,000		
GDP per capita	760,534		
Total central government expenditure (millions)	2,193,724		

a. LCU is local currency unit.

1. Staff estimates of wage adjustment are included, allocated according to the ratio of defense to nondefense personal emoluments.

Sources: IMF RED tables; and WB *World Development Indicators* database for population.

antipoverty programs is not as straightforward a proposition as it may seem, since civil servants often support poor, extended families.

The government, the Fund, and the Bank agree that it is important to try to contain the across-the-board wage increases demanded by the unions each year, while raising compensation for senior management.

5. Need for Including Civil Service Reforms in PRSC and PRGF Programs?

Though it is virtually impossible to propose expenditure adjustments while leaving the wage bill untouched, it is also unrealistic simply to insist that wage increases be denied when political pressures are so strong. As such, a well-designed reform program—including some mix of retrenchments and moderate wage increases—should be a component of PRGF programs.

For the past three years PSCAP has been part of a series of adjustment operations. The most recent operation will provide complementary capacity building for a future PRSC. The budgeting process itself should be improved by getting the cabinet involved in setting the budgetary priorities as a result of the support given by PSCAP to the introduction of the medium-term expenditure framework (MTEF) and the linkages established between policy and resources.

6. Benchmarks for the Future. How Will Progress Be Monitored?

Previous conditionality requiring the retrenchment of a given number of civil servants each year has been replaced by a focus on the broader goals of civil service reform. Benchmarks in the new program include (a) progress in pay reform, such as monetization of benefits; (b) financial management and accountability; (c) rationalization of roles, functions, and structures for ministries and agencies; (d) establishment of effective payroll and control systems; and (e) transparency measures.

Notes

1. The issues paper was based on 11 country cases illustrating recent Bank- and Fund-supported civil service reforms: Benin, Bolivia, Cambodia, the FYR of Macedonia, Mali, Mongolia, Pakistan, the Russian Federation, Tanzania, the Republic of Yemen, and Zambia.

2. Prepared by the FAD of the IMF and the Public Sector Group of the Poverty Reduction and Economic Management (PREM) Network in the Bank, with assistance from Fund Area Departments and Bank country teams. This is a staff discussion paper. It is not for decision, and has not been endorsed by senior management in the Bank or the Fund.

3. See "Strengthening IMF–World Bank Collaboration on Country Programs and Conditionality" (August 23, 2001) http://www.imf.org/external/np/pdr/cond/2001/eng/collab/coll.htm.

4. The 11 sample countries are: Benin, Bolivia, Cambodia, the FYR of Macedonia, Mali, Mongolia, Pakistan, the Russian Federation, Tanzania, the Republic of Yemen, and Zambia.

5. Data on public employment for local governments were available for only 6 of the 11 case studies. In many countries, subnational governments could constitute a substantial part of public employment, such as employment in health and education. Given the significance and complexities of public employment issues in education and health, it may be necessary to address reforms of these sectors separately from the reform of general civil service administration.

6. The case studies, in focusing on core central government employees, have not emphasized the parallel work that may be taking place in the health and education sectors (see endnote 5). Teachers or medical professionals usually constitute a majority of civilian central government staff with direct service delivery responsibility. There are also many parallel reforms in subnational government currently under way in these two sectors.

7. Per capita GDP itself can be a questionable measure when labor participation rates are low and much of the economy is informal.

8. The PRGF provides medium-term assistance to countries where poverty reduction is the cornerstone of the growth-oriented economic strategy. It is based on a comprehensive, nationally owned PRSP prepared by the borrowing country and endorsed in their respective areas of responsibility by the Boards of the Fund and Bank as the basis for the institutions' concessional loans and for relief under the enhanced HIPC Initiative.

9. The EFF provides medium-term assistance to members with (a) an economy suffering a serious payments imbalance relating to structural maladjustments in production and trade and where price and cost distortions have been widespread; or (b) an economy characterized by slow growth and an inherently weak balance of payments position that prevents pursuit of an active development policy. The length of an EFF arrangement is typically three years, and disbursement is conditional on the borrower's meeting specified performance requirements, including structural reforms.

10. In particular, the availability of an integrated computerized payroll system can be very useful in identifying ghost workers, irregular wage drift, irregular hiring, and wage arrears.

11. Pension reform was subsequently dropped as a structural benchmark in the Republic of Yemen.

12. See "Strengthening IMF–World Bank Collaboration on Country Programs and Conditionality" (August 23, 2001) http://www.imf.org/external/np/pdr/cond/2001/eng/collab/coll.htm.

13. Adjustment loans have a short-term focus (1 to 3 years), and provide quick-disbursing assistance to countries with external financing needs, to support structural reforms in a sector or the economy as a whole. They support the policy and institutional changes needed to create an environment conducive to sustained and equitable growth.

14. Investment loans have a long-term focus (5 to 10 years) and finance goods, works, and services in support of economic and social development projects in a broad range of sectors.

15. Programmatic loans are arranged as a series of operations that support a medium-term government program of policy reforms and institution building.

16. Employment in subnational government has been increasing (particularly in Latin America), partially offsetting the reduction in central government staffing.

17. See "Strengthening IMF–World Bank Collaboration on Country Programs and Conditionality" (August 23, 2001) http://www.imf.org/external/np/pdr/cond/2001/eng/collab/coll.htm.

18. See "Strengthening IMF–World Bank Collaboration on Country Programs and Conditionality" (August 23, 2001) http://www.imf.org/external/np/pdr/cond/2001/eng/collab/coll.htm.

19. See http://www1.worldbank.org/publicsector/civilservice/surveys.htm.

20. See http://www1.worldbank.org/publicsector/civilservice/cross.htm.

21. These core civil service reform operations are defined as those that directly target employment, pay, and working practices of civilian central

government, excluding reforms that affect the employment arrangements for professional health personnel, primary and secondary school teachers, police, armed forces, and staffs of state-owned enterprises. See http://www1.worldbank.org/publicsector/civilservice/cross.htm#1 for further details of employment categories.

22. Two important reforms have been enacted. In 1987 state hiring of all university graduates was abolished. In education (a stronghold of the unions), a reform was enacted so that new hires are contract employees (with wages a little more than half those in the civil service), who are offered a career perspective through late entry to the civil service (after 10 years of service and based on a competitive exam).

23. *Wage and Salary Structure: Final Report,* Team, June 1997, for the Institutional Development for Public Administration project.

Index

Note: *f* indicates figures, *n* indicates notes, and *t* indicates tables